John Wesley Powell

John
WESLEY

POWELL

HIS LIFE AND LEGACY

James M. Aton

Bonneville Books
Salt Lake City

Bonneville Books is a joint imprint of The University of Utah Press and the J. Willard Marriott Library at The University of Utah.

Copyright © 2010 by The University of Utah Press. All rights reserved.

Chapter 1 is a slightly revised version of *John Wesley Powell*, published in Boise State University's Western Writers Series in 1994. Chapter 3 is a revised version of "Inventing John Wesley Powell: The Major, His Admirers, and Cash-Register Dams in the Colorado River Basin," Distinguished Faculty Lecture No. 9, 1988, at Southern Utah State College.

Bonneville **Books**

Salt Lake City

The Bonneville Books colophon depicts a Quetzalcoatlus, a giant pterosaur with a fifty-foot wing-span, and is courtesy of Frank DeCourten.

Bonneville Books is a joint imprint of The University of Utah Press and the J. Willard Marriott Library at The University of Utah.

LIBRARY OF CONGRESS CATALOGING-IN-PUBLICATION DATA

14 13 12 11 10   1 2 3 4 5

Aton, James M., 1949-
    John Wesley Powell : his life and legacy / by James
    M. Aton.
      p. cm.
Includes bibliographical references and index.
ISBN 978-0-87480-992-3 (pbk. : alk. paper)
1. Powell, John Wesley, 1834-1902. 2. Scientists—United
States—Biography. 3. Naturalists—United States—Biogra-
phy. 4. Powell, John Wesley, 1834-1902—Criticism and inter-
pretation. 5. Powell, John Wesley, 1834-1902--Influence. I.
Title.
Q143.P8A865 2010
917.91'3044092—dc22
                                          2009046587

Cover map courtesy of Library of Congress, Geography and Map Division.
Cover photo of Tau-gu and John Wesley Powell courtesy of Special Collections, J. Willard Marriot Library, University of Utah.

For Carrie, the love of my life

Contents

Acknowledgments

I am indebted to numerous people who read parts of this manuscript, supported the research, or provided technical assistance: Tom Birch, Kyle Bishop, Michael P. Cohen, Glenda Cotter, Rodney D. Decker, Peter H. DeLafosse, Mark W. T. Harvey, Lilly Jensen, David W. Lee, James H. Maguire, Paula Mitchell, Richard Quartaroli, Amanda Utzman, Jill Wilks, and Donald Worster. All errors are mine alone.

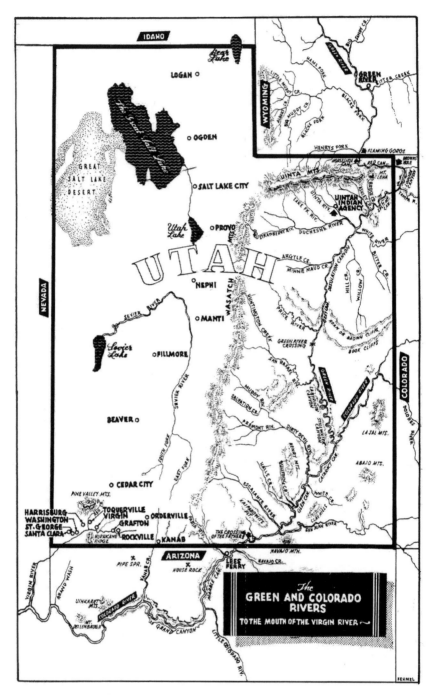

Map of the Green and Colorado rivers. Used by permission, Utah State Historical Society, all rights reserved.

1   Biography

As John Wesley Powell stood on the banks of the muddy Green River on 24 May 1869 ready to start his now-famous journey down the river, he knew that a successful trip was by no means assured. In fact, despite his planning, it was still a crap shoot, a roll of the dice. But he probably knew that success would bring him fame. He also might have guessed that he could write a popular account of the trip. And, always confident of his abilities, he might have surmised that this trip could catapult him into a position in government science. But surely none of his men foresaw as much. Nor probably did his wife or supporters in Illinois and Washington, D.C., foresee Powell's future unfolding in so many directions. In the spring of 1869 Powell was a virtual unknown, a wild card in science, exploration, and adventure literature. Twenty years later he stood at or near the height of all those fields.

John Wesley Powell: explorer, writer, geologist, anthropologist, land planner, bureaucrat. Which one do we focus on? Do we concentrate on the trailblazer who explored the last blank spot on our nation's map? Do we look at the artist who wrote one of the great, real-life adventure stories in American literature, *Exploration of the*

Colorado River? Or do we turn to the scientist who produced significant works in geology, anthropology, and land policy, such as *Report on the Lands of the Arid Region*? In fact, one cannot ignore any part of his multifaceted life. Powell was a polymath, a jack of many trades who excelled at them all. His divergent interests resemble one of those braided streambeds in his beloved canyon country, branching out in many directions, but ultimately beginning and ending in the same stream. Few men or women in the nineteenth century pursued as many avenues of intellectual study and fewer still performed so well. And John Wesley Powell started from a distinct disadvantage: he had little formal education.

Powell's story in many ways reads like the story of other famous, frontier-bred Americans. His parents, Joseph and Mary Powell, immigrated to New York from England in 1830. A Methodist preacher, Joseph Powell was a "diligent reader, a terse speaker, a sound thinker; honest, precise, and devout."[1] The father's severity was offset by the mother's gentleness. Later in life Powell would recall his mother with more affection than he felt for his father. Suffice it to say that both parents had some education, good minds, and high moral principles, all of which their son would benefit from and build upon.

Joseph Powell possessed religious zeal and a restless spirit. Gradually he pushed the family west across New York. At Mount Morris on 24 March 1834, his second son, John Wesley "Wes," was born. After eight peripatetic years in New York, the family moved to Jackson in southern Ohio. Like many border communities, Jackson was a hotbed of debate over slavery. Joseph Powell argued actively and publicly against it. It was this public stand that forced Wes out of the local schools, where his classmates called him "abolitionist" and threw rocks at him. He ended up studying with his father's friend George Crookham, probably the most learned man in Jackson County.

The three-hundred-fifty-pound Crookham offered to educate Wes along with four other young men. Thereafter followed a course of studies and pedagogical methodology that Powell would later use with his students in Illinois. We now call it the "field trip." Crookham and young Powell would amble around places like Salt Creek Gorge, with Crookham illuminating all the natural history along the way.

Teacher and pupil also dug in the Hopewell culture mounds that dot the southern Ohio landscape. Later Powell reflected on this educational experience as one of the most important influences on his life. Unfortunately, their association ended in the mid-1840s when pro-slavery advocates burned Crookham's schoolhouse. Shortly thereafter, in 1846, feeling the same pressure, Joseph Powell moved the family farther west to a farm in Walworth County, Wisconsin, near the Illinois border.[2] By this time, at age twelve, Powell's intellectual interests in natural history and ethnology had been fired and stoked. Now ensued a long period of self-education.

If southern Ohio had been the golden days of Powell's education, southern Wisconsin and later northern Illinois proved to be the school of hard knocks. But no evidence exists that Powell resented his teenage years. Indeed, his early life farming in Ohio, Wisconsin, and Illinois must have agreed with him because he spent the better part of his professional life with the United States Geological Survey and Bureau of Ethnology trying to help other Americans—Anglo and Indian—achieve the same kind of agrarian life.

As soon as Joseph Powell acquired land in Walworth County, he struck out to preach on the ministerial circuit; he entrusted the breaking of the land and farming to twelve-year-old Wes. Somehow Wes, his mother, and his ten-year-old brother, Bram, managed to do it all: by the third year they had cleared sixty acres and were hauling wheat to market. But Wes hungered for book learning. Like his future commander-in-chief, Abraham Lincoln, Powell got books any way he could. He spent those years reading widely in history, science, and philosophy. His favorite was John Bunyan's *A Pilgrim's Progress*.

In the 1850s, after quarrelling with his father over the elder Powell's insistence that Wes become a minister, Powell left home and began the first of a series of high school teaching jobs in Illinois. He also squeezed in a few terms as a college student. In the summers he collected fossils on the Ohio, Mississippi, Illinois, and other midwestern rivers. Powell wanted to be a scientist, and while his formal training lagged, the field knowledge and self-confidence he acquired on these trips proved immeasurable. No doubt he also learned many valuable lessons about water travel and watercraft which later helped him in 1869 on his famous voyage down the Green and Colorado rivers.

When war came in the winter of 1860–1861, Powell promptly enlisted and within a month rose to the rank of second lieutenant. Stationed at Cape Girardeau, Missouri, he came under the command of General John C. Frémont. One can only speculate about what Powell, if he did gain access, asked Frémont about the West. In the fall of 1861 Powell received from newly appointed commander Ulysses S. Grant a one-week leave of absence to marry his half-cousin, Emma Dean of Detroit. Powell and his bride rushed back to Missouri to find that he had been commissioned a captain in the artillery.

The following April at the Battle of Shiloh, he took a bullet in his right arm. As was standard medical practice at the time, the battlefield surgeon, William Medcalfe of Olney, Illinois, promptly amputated the arm two inches below the elbow. Although he recovered and returned to active duty, Powell suffered pain in his stub for the rest of his life.

Powell distinguished himself at Vicksburg and elsewhere under Generals Grant and Sherman, and in 1865 returned to civilian life in Wheaton, Illinois, with the rank of major. Several opportunities for employment quickly presented themselves, most notably a county clerkship of DuPage County, worth the lucrative sum of five thousand dollars per year. Illinois Wesleyan University in Bloomington countered with a professorship in geology, worth one thousand dollars per year. Not surprisingly, the Major chose science over politics. Eventually, however, science would lead him back to politics, but on a national stage.

When Powell began to teach science—his duties included not just geology but many of the sciences—he remembered the kind of field study to which Crookham had introduced him. At every opportunity he led his students into the surrounding fields and forests to gather plants, search for animals, and collect rocks. Although he probably did not realize it, Powell was revolutionizing the teaching of science. And when he took a group of students on an extended field trip to the Rocky Mountains, it was one of the first such trips of its kind in American higher education.[3]

Following a short stint at Illinois Wesleyan, Powell moved to neighboring Illinois State Normal University. He also became secretary of the Illinois Natural History Society and curator of its museum. In that latter capacity, Powell promptly decided to increase the museum's collections. Spurred by the wanderlust that had characterized his father's life and his own adolescence, Powell organized a scientific expedition to Colorado. Composed mostly of students and a few faculty colleagues, the expedition received funding from a variety of sources. Powell's old commander, Ulysses S. Grant, arranged for him to buy rations from government commissaries at government rates. All the students and other expedition members agreed to pay their own expenses, and Powell obtained five hundred dollars from the Illinois Natural History Museum. Various railroad lines gave the group free passage, and the Smithsonian loaned him the necessary scientific equipment in return for any topographic readings his party made. Powell also used some of his own money to help finance the group's expenses. Until he won appropriation from Congress after the successful 1869 trip down the Colorado, Powell financed three seasons in the West by this patchwork method.[4]

Green but enthusiastic, Powell's party tumbled into Denver in July of 1867, and shortly thereafter climbed Pike's and Lincoln peaks. Emma Powell, nearly always with her husband on his explorations, was one of the first women to climb Pike's Peak. The Powell group spent the better part of the summer collecting specimens of all sorts for the museum. In Denver, Powell met O. G. Howland of the *Rocky Mountain News* and Jack Sumner, brother-in-law of the newspaper's editor, William Byers. When the Major left Colorado in the fall of 1867 to return to Illinois, he had formulated a plan to explore the last blank spot on the map—the canyons of the Colorado River—and had secured the services of Howland, Sumner, Billy Hawkins, and William Dunn to help him the following season.[5] These men would form the nucleus of the river expedition two years later.

Powell spent the winter of 1867–1868 teaching, sorting through his collection, and organizing a return trip to Colorado. He also went east to solicit support from the Smithsonian and from Congress for his proposed exploration of the Colorado River. As Smithsonian secretary Joseph Henry explained in a letter of introduction to James A. Garfield, then the most influential member of the House, Powell's survey of the Colorado River would give special attention to the possibilities of irrigation in this arid region. With but one season in the West, Powell was already formulating ideas about arid lands agriculture. These ideas flowered into a classic statement of environmental history, *Report on the Lands of the Arid Region* (1878; although the second printing in 1879 is considered the definitive edition; hereafter *Arid Lands Report*). He later wrote that he first became interested in reclamation and arid lands agriculture while discussing the future of the West with William Byers of the *Rocky Mountain News*, soon-to-be Vice-President Schuyler Colfax, Samuel Bowles of the *Springfield Republican*, and numerous other luminaries he camped with in Middle Park, Colorado, in 1868.[6]

Powell's second expedition to Colorado in 1868, called the Rocky Mountain Scientific Exploring Expedition, boasted three professional biologists among its twenty-one members. The party spent three months collecting for the museum, taking measurements, and studying the Rocky Mountain flora and fauna. Powell himself encountered a band of Yampatika (or White River) Utes, and this rekindled an interest in native cultures that he first acquired through Crookham in southern Ohio. The Major began to study their language and thus began another life-long endeavor. This one would eventually lead him not only to direct the Bureau of Ethnology, but also to help establish anthropology as a federally funded science.

When the rest of his party traveled east in the fall, Powell moved his camp farther west to the lower White River near present-day Meeker, Colorado. With the core of his next year's river crew, plus his brother Walter, Powell spent part of December and January exploring the Yampa River as well as the Green River near Brown's Hole. Otherwise he visited with the local Utes, studying their language and recording their stories and customs. The budding anthropologist could not have had a better situation for study. In early spring Powell hopped a train to Chicago where he and master boat builder Thomas Bagley designed the boats (modeled after the "ferry tenders" Powell had seen on midwestern rivers and lakes) that would carry him into "the great unknown."[7]

Because Green River, Wyoming, lay on the recently completed transcontinental railroad line, Powell decided to start his river adventure from there. Besides what scant information Powell might have gleaned about Green River from fur trappers by word-of-mouth, little was known about that river and nothing about the Colorado. A miner named James White claimed he went through the Grand Canyon in 1867. After being dragged off a raft at Callville, Nevada, near death, White said that he had floated down from near the San Juan River. Although Powell sought out White, possibly near Fort Bridger, he came away unconvinced that White had actually passed through the Grand Canyon. Many river historians today think White's story is probably accurate.[8]

Either way, Powell had very little to go on, especially for the Colorado River itself. What he heard from Anglo and Indian alike was tales of horror: of a current that disappeared beneath the ground, of canyon walls a mile high, of great waterfalls. And while an element of truth hangs on all those fables, the prospect of a waterfall seemed the most real threat. Yet Powell the scientist already understood enough about the key to Colorado Plateau geology—erosion—not to fear waterfalls. Years later Harvard geologist W. H. Brewer asked him if he wasn't afraid of such falls as he planned his river trip. Powell replied, "Have you never seen the river? It is the muddiest river you ever saw.... I was convinced that the canyon was old enough, and the muddy water swift enough and gritty enough to have worn down all the falls to mere rapids."[9] He was correct, as he was to be about most basic Plateau Province geology.

The crew that Powell assembled in Green River hardly qualified as scientists. In fact none of them had any scientific training whatsoever. What O. G. Howland, Seneca Howland, Jack Sumner, William Dunn, Billy Hawkins, George Bradley, Walter Powell, and Andy Hall could claim, however, was experience in the outdoors. A last-minute addition, Frank Goodman, could claim only enthusiasm. Whatever science was accomplished on the trip would be the Major's responsibility.

Much has been written about Powell's motley crew, about his poorly designed boats, and about his overbearing military demeanor throughout the trip. Suffice it to say that Powell's crew handled the difficulties of river travel well enough, even if they did not contribute much to science. The boats themselves proved they could make it through big water when they had to. As for Powell's martinet-like behavior, undoubtedly he sometimes pulled too hard on his men's strings.

When Powell's men pushed off from Green River on 24 May 1869, many of the locals turned out to see them off, some to shout warnings. With nine other men and four boats, Powell had stowed provisions calculated to last ten months. Moreover, for scientific work he had "two sextants, four chronometers, a number of barometers, thermometers, compasses, and other instruments."[10]

Walter Powell and George Bradley manned *Kitty Clyde's Sister*; Billy Hawkins and Andy Hall oared the *Maid of the Canyon*; O. G. Howland, Seneca Howland, and Frank Goodman rode in the *No Name*; while Powell, Jack Sumner, and Bill Dunn led in the lighter *Emma Dean*. This last boat measured sixteen feet, was constructed of pine, and was built for the speed a scout boat required. The other three boats boasted oak frames, stretched twenty-one feet, and contained water-tight compartments fore and aft. During the first sixty miles of canyons, the crew experienced a few minor mishaps, but on 2 June when they floated into the meadows of Brown's Park, their spirits soared. Six days later, in Lodore Canyon, disaster struck.

Numerous versions of what happened have come down, but all accounts agree that the *No Name*, with Goodman and the Howlands aboard, missed the signal to pull over above a big rapid. The boat then hit a rock and careened. The men lost their oars, and shortly thereafter the craft hit another rock and split in two. All three men managed to grab onto some rocks in midstream. After some fancy oaring by Sumner in the *Emma Dean*, the swimmers, shaken but unharmed, all grabbed onto his boat and made it to shore. Powell wore the only lifejacket on the trip.

Named Disaster Falls, this rapid not only cost the expedition a boat, many food provisions, and scientific instruments, it also put a damper on the trip. According to some accounts, it sowed the seed of enmity between Powell and the Howlands.[11] Whatever the truth of the latter item, the expedition now suffered in many ways, especially in the amount of time they had to measure, map, and geologize. Although they recovered some instruments and food downstream, the accident caused, as Bradley put it, "a serious loss to us and we are rather low-spirrited [sic] tonight."[12]

Nothing calamitous happened through the rest of Lodore, Whirlpool, and Split Mountain canyons, but when the expedition reached the Duchesne River in the Uinta Basin, Goodman left the trip. Major Powell walked forty miles to the Uinta Indian Agency at Whiterocks to replenish food supplies, but returned with only three hundred pounds of flour. In all likelihood, the agency was low on supplies, and Powell anyway had little money to purchase such.

For the better part of July the men toiled through the rapids of Desolation and Gray canyons, floated the smooth water of Labyrinth and Stillwater canyons, and in 100-degree heat portaged the big drops of Cataract Canyon. Still, they made it through. Glen Canyon brought cooler temperatures and relief from the rapids, but the party could not linger to enjoy the beauties of that now-flooded canyon. The men wanted to press on, even though Powell, always the scientist, insisted on stopping to take latitude and longitude measurements. Bradley seemed to speak for the whole group when he wrote, "[W]e are willing to face starvation if necessary to do it [take measurements] but further than that he should not ask us to wait and he must go on soon now or the consequences will be different from what he anticipates."[13] In his zeal to survey the territory successfully, Powell sometimes ignored his men's needs. In fact, he seemed not to notice the frayed nerves and sinking morale.

Early August saw the group pass from Glen Canyon into Marble Canyon, and that meant many rapids and more portaging. Yet despite the slow pace and hard work, Powell, Bradley, and Sumner all commented in their journals on the many beautiful spots in Marble Canyon. Bradley called the towering waterfall at Vasey's Paradise "the prettiest sight of the whole trip."[14] Regarding the polished limestone walls, Powell was moved to write, "And now the scenery is on a grand scale.... Through a cleft in the wall the sun shines on this pavement and it gleams in iridescent beauty."[15]

When the group arrived at the Flax, or Little Colorado River on 10 August, Powell commanded the party to stop a few days to take barometric, latitude, and longitude readings and to explore nearby Ancestral Puebloan ruins. But as Bradley wrote in his journal, the men were "uneasy and discontented and anxious to move on."[16]

Once in the Grand Canyon proper, the party faced some of the worst rapids in North America. In the first forty miles they tried to portage many of the rapids, but in some cases had to run fearsome drops now known as Unkar, Nevills, Hance, Sockdolager, Grapevine, Horn Creek, Granite, Hermit, Tuna Creek, and Sapphire—all dangerous rapids currently rated between 5 and 9. Midway through that horrid stretch they stopped on 16 August at Silver (later Bright Angel) Creek to fish, hunt bighorn sheep, patch boats, and reshape oars. To add to their troubles, rain brought many sleepless nights since their now-shredded ponchos provided little shelter. Although cold, hungry, and sick, Bradley was "still in good spirits."[17]

From this point on it appears that Powell recognized their dire situation and curtailed his insistence on geologizing. Nevertheless, he continued to observe the broad outlines of the canyon's geology. His notes from this part of the trip show his grasp of the basic history of Inner Gorge geology. Still, it was everything that the men could do just to make their way down the canyon on what little food they had. On 26 August the party found a patch of corn and squash at Spring or Indian Canyon, probably planted by Shivwits Paiute or Hualapai Indians. Ripe enough to eat, the squash provided a welcome relief from a constant diet of unleavened biscuits, coffee, and dried apples.

But the next day they reached what Bradley and others agreed was "the worst rapid yet seen."[18] Separation Rapid, as it has since become known, proved the expedition's undoing. Pages and pages have been written, analyzing what took place there. Some believe everything Powell said in his book. On the detractors' side stand Otis Marston, Robert B. Stanton, Julius Stone, Michael Ghiglieri, and others. They assert that Separation merely exacerbated long-festering tensions which started at Disaster Falls and worsened because of Powell's overbearing manner.

Powell himself, in an account written five years after the event, depicts the parting as tearful and in good friendship. His actual trip journal—always extremely brief—merely says, "Boys left us." Jack Sumner reports that the Howlands and Dunn left, though he mentions nothing in the way of acrimonious feelings. Bradley, who wrote expansively in his journal and never feared criticizing the Major there, wrote, "There is discontent in camp tonight and I fear some of the party will take to the mountains but hope not. This is decidedly the darkest day of the trip but I don't despair yet." Then the next day he said, "They left us with good feelings though we deeply regret their loss for they are as fine fellows as I have ever had the good fortune to meet."[19]

Whatever the exact circumstances, whatever the exact mood in camp, the three men clearly feared for their lives and thought they stood a better chance of climbing out of the canyon and walking to the Mormon settlements of St. George or Toquerville. They never made it. Some Shivwits Indians, who mistook them for miners who had killed a Hualapai woman on the south side of the river, killed Powell's men. That, at least, is the story Powell heard the next year when he visited the Shivwits area with Mormon scout Jacob Hamblin. A few historians have suggested that the men were killed by Mormons who mistook them for federal agents searching for polygamists.[20] No one knows for sure how Powell's men died.

After leaving the three men, Powell and the other five men rowed successfully through Separation and Lava Cliff rapids (they now lie under Lake Mead). In two days they passed beyond Grand Wash Cliffs and floated to the mouth of the Virgin River. There, some Mormon settlers spotted them, took them in, and fed them. Powell and his brother departed for Salt Lake City while Sumner, Bradley, Hawkins, and Hall pushed on down the Colorado. While Powell's account certainly ranks with the great American adventure stories, these four remaining men were the true adventurers.

Many have said that Powell made it through the canyon by sheer luck, and he acknowledged as much himself years later. But Powell has endured another rap: that the 1869 expedition accomplished little science. This is both true and false. In tangible terms the statement is accurate. No map was drawn. If Howland carried one out, and it is doubtful he did, it disappeared when he died on the Shivwits Plateau. No rock samples came out of the canyon, and no scientific monographs appeared right after. But in the larger sense, Powell accomplished much. As his geological notes indicate, Powell's eye took in the broad geological outlines of the canyon country. Already he grasped its basic structure: the river preceded the canyons and then cut them as the plateau rose.

These and other ideas about erosion he bequeathed to his later collaborators, the brilliant geologists Grove Karl Gilbert and Clarence E. Dutton. In the process these three men helped rewrite aspects of the field of geology. Powell made his greatest direct contribution with the terms he introduced to describe Colorado Plateau drainage systems. In his *Geology of the Eastern Uinta Mountains* (1876) he classifies three kinds of river valleys: "antecedent," "consequent," and "superimposed."[21] Moreover, he introduced the term "base level of erosion"—the level below which dry land cannot be eroded. In these and other conceptions, Powell laid the foundations, as Harvard geologist William Morris Davis said, "of what may be fairly called the American school of geomorphology."[22]

With these ideas about the Colorado River country in mind, Powell returned to Illinois a national hero. His river exploits had captured the fancy of an eastern public starved for news of western adventuring. Powell promptly hit the lecture circuit, mostly in the Midwest. Although his voice hardly boomed like Ralph Waldo Emerson's baritone, he lectured the way he later wrote—with clarity and precision. These skills would help him years later when testifying before Congress. Also, in talking about his trip, he was shaping, refining, and expanding the story that would become his most famous book, *Exploration of the Colorado River of the West*.

Powell's immediate problem in 1870, though, was funding. To continue his survey over a number of seasons, he needed to show Congress tangible scientific results. And a second expedition would produce what the first one did not—a map and scientific publications. But Powell knew how to ride the crest of his fame and parlay it into financial support. Once again he sought the aid of Joseph Henry and Spencer Baird of the Smithsonian and Representative James A. Garfield. Largely through their influence, Congress appropriated $10,000 and $12,000 for the next two years for "The Geographical and Topographical Survey of the Colorado River of the West."[23] Although it later acquired different titles, it has always been known as the "Powell Survey."

During the summer and fall of 1870, Powell returned to Utah with two goals: find routes down the Colorado to cache food for the upcoming 1871 expedition, and determine the fate of the three men who reportedly died on the Shivwits Plateau. In both of these endeavors he enlisted the aid of Jacob Hamblin, the Mormon buckskin apostle. Thereafter, the two traveled to Fort Defiance in Arizona to help negotiate between the Mormons and the Navajos. Largely through Powell's efforts, both sides signed the Treaty of Fort Defiance on 3 November 1870. This ended a decade of strife between the Mormons and the Athabascan-speaking Indians from the Four Corners area.

For his second expedition Powell once again neglected to hire any noted scientists. Still, his crew of mostly fellow teachers and students constituted a significant step up in professionalism from the first trip. Professor Almon H. Thompson, a brother-in-law, served as the geographer and second in charge. Frederick S. Dellenbaugh, also a distant relative and a talented artist, later became one of the most prominent Colorado River historians and wrote the only account of the trip, *A Canyon Voyage* (1908). An outsider, E. O. Beaman of New York, came along as the trip's professional photographer. Another outsider, John K. Hillers, signed on in Salt Lake City as a boatman when winter snows delayed Jack Sumner. Hillers went on to great fame as a U.S. Geological Survey photographer, a skill he picked up on the 1871–1872 expedition. The others were relatives, colleagues, or students of Powell's. This expedition proved one of the most documented in nineteenth-century western exploration: nearly every member of the crew kept a detailed journal.

Powell's passion for river exploration on the second trip clearly did not match that of the first trip. For various reasons he left the expedition numerous times before it reached Lees Ferry in late fall of 1871. Powell left Thompson in charge, and the geographer held the sometimes grumbling crew together while accomplishing important topographical work. He not only produced the first map of this previously blank spot, he also "discovered" the United States' last major river, the Escalante, and the last mountain range, the Henrys, named after the Smithsonian's Joseph Henry.

In mid-August of 1872, when Powell continued river exploration below Lees Ferry, he had been a father for eleven months. Mary Dean Powell was born in Salt Lake City in September 1871, and by December she, Emma Powell, and Thompson's wife Nell had traveled to Kanab where the survey party had set up winter camp. Ironically, Powell had also recently become fatherless. Reverend Joseph Powell had died in December. And fortunately for Wes, he had long since forgiven his son for becoming a scientist instead of a minister. The son of a minister, Powell eventually became what Wallace Stegner called "The High Priest of Science" for late nineteenth-century America.

From 17 August to 8 September the party toiled through the Grand Canyon to the mouth of Kanab Creek. Numerous flips and rising waters convinced Powell and Thompson that navigating the rest of the canyon would accomplish little science. As Dellenbaugh said, "We were in the field to accomplish certain work not to perform a spectacular feat."[24] Compounding these difficulties, a message arrived from Jacob Hamblin stating that the Shivwits Indians planned to ambush the party in the Lower Grand Canyon area. Therefore, Thompson determined he could map the rest of the canyon from various points on the North Rim. On 10 September the party tied up the *Nellie Powell*, the *Cañonita*, and the *Emma Dean* and packed out Kanab Creek north to the Arizona Strip.

Now Powell went straight from Kanab Creek to Congress and requested $20,000 for the 1873 season. He wanted to resign from his teaching position at Normal, take up permanent residence in Washington, and direct a more or less permanent survey. He succeeded. Moreover, with funds from the sale of the expedition's photographs, he purchased a house at 910 M St. NW in the nation's capital. In doing so he fully committed himself to a life in federal science.

In addition to directing his survey, largely from Washington, Powell received a special commission with Indian agent G. W. Ingalls to investigate the problems of the Numic-speaking Indians (the Ute, Shoshone, and Paiute tribes of Utah and eastern Nevada). Powell took up the assignment with relish. It allowed him to complete his series of Numic vocabularies, record mythologies and social institutions, and collect for the Smithsonian artifacts relating to Numic dress, food, arts, warfare, and ceremonies. Since his first encounter with the Yampatika or White River Utes, his professional interests had been changing from geology to ethnology.

Between intermittent field work in 1873 and 1874 and work in Washington, Powell hired geologists Grove Karl Gilbert and Clarence E. Dutton. As Wallace Stegner has said, "During the years they worked together, they were probably the most brilliant geological team in the business."[25] Even though Powell's interests at the time were moving toward ethnology, he had formed many of the overarching ideas about canyon country geology. These concepts he gave freely to Gilbert and Dutton. Their combined efforts represent, no doubt, a richer substitute for the comprehensive work on the area Powell originally envisioned.

Gilbert's *Report on the Geology of the Henry Mountains* (1877) appeared as a Powell Survey monograph and stands as the classic statement on arid lands erosion and laccoliths (bubble mountains formed of sedimentary layers domed upward by underlying lava). Gilbert also contributed to Powell's *Arid Lands Report*, served as ranking geologist for the U.S. Geological Survey, and was Powell's closest friend.

Whereas Gilbert's biographer, Stephen Pyne, describes Gilbert as an "engine of research," Dutton was something of an aesthete, in the mode of his contemporary and Yale classmate, Clarence King. When reading Dutton's *Tertiary History of the Grand Cañon District* (1882) and *Report on the Geology of the High Plateaus of Utah* (1880), one sees not only a superb geologist working out theories of erosion and volcanism, but also a fine prose stylist and nature writer. Dutton's descriptions of Point Sublime, Zion Canyon, the Markagunt Plateau, the Escalante country, and other grand scenes in southern Utah and northern Arizona are today studied in literature classes as some of the best nineteenth-century nature writing.

In addition to Gilbert and Dutton, Powell hired two artists whose work greatly enhanced the later Powell Survey publications. The first, Thomas Moran, had already achieved great fame for his Yellowstone paintings while working for the Hayden Survey. His woodcuts appeared in the 1875 edition of Powell's *Exploration*. Later his art would help provide a visual equivalent for Dutton's lush words in the *Tertiary History*. Moran became known as one of America's best landscape painters.

Lesser known than Moran but increasingly recognized for his genius in portraying the canyon country was William H. Holmes. Wallace Stegner claims that Holmes's detailed illustrations of canyon country geology "represent the highest point to which topographical illustration ever reached in this country."[26] In our day Holmes's "art without falsification" is usually the first choice of editors looking for a nineteenth-century illustration of the Colorado Plateau. Like his boss, Holmes possessed many talents and exercised them well. He began as a scientific illustrator, became a geologist, an ethnologist, and a curator of the Field and National Museums. He also headed the Bureau of Ethnology and the National Gallery.[27]

As Thompson and Powell's other men finished their reconnaissance of the Colorado River country in the early 1870s, the Major felt pressure from his benefactors, Baird of the Smithsonian and Representative Garfield, to publish a report of his explorations. Further funding, they argued, would depend on it. Thus Powell put form to a five-year-old story he had been telling and had partially written. In June of 1874 he submitted his first manuscript—*Exploration of the Colorado River of the West*. The government published it the following year. As *Exploration* saw print and gained a large readership, Powell finished revising *The Geology of the Eastern Portion of the Uinta Mountains*. Taking up where the second part of *Exploration* left off, the Uinta Mountains report further propounded Powell's theories about uplift and erosion.

Although this book was the last geology that Powell would publish, it meshes with his later work on reclamation and ethnology. To understand Powell's basic philosophy in all his various scientific work, one must understand Darwin and evolution. Powell fully grasped and incorporated Darwin's theories into his own work. When the Major looked at the geology and physiography of the canyon country, he saw the gradual evolution of a landscape, hastened by uniform processes of erosion and uplift. Similarly, when he studied Native Americans, Powell borrowed from Darwin's evolution theory and applied it to society and culture. Thus, in the tribes that he studied, Powell perceived a gradual evolution of these societies from "savagery" to "barbarism" to "civilization." Likewise, when he studied the problems of water in the arid region, he would also use Darwin's idea of "adaption." Even though it might appear to some that Powell's mind was moving in many directions at once, the ideas that informed his work are in large part Darwin's. And while many American scientists interpreted and followed Darwin, perhaps Powell applied the British biologist's ideas as thoroughly as anyone.[28]

In the decade after his first venture west, Powell made almost thirty trips to the Rocky Mountain and Great Basin areas.[29] The West had changed greatly in that post-Civil War decade, and Powell did not like everything he saw happening there. For every example of cooperation he found with people like the Mormons, he found ten examples of greed, exploitation, and environmental ignorance. From the beginning in 1867, Powell, being a good Jeffersonian agrarian, felt that his survey should map the country so that its settlers could know what to expect in terms of water, forest, and grazing resources. Unlike the King Survey, which worked indirectly for mining industries, the Powell Survey oriented itself toward populist, agrarian concerns. The young man who grew up farming in the Midwest envisioned a West where other Americans could do the same. But one crucial difference separated Powell's midwestern agrarian experience and the western pioneer's: aridity. In 1867, Powell saw immediately that water dictated the terms of western settlement. Yet between 1867 and 1894 he had to fight any number of myths about western agriculture. His first attempt to debunk those myths appeared in his *Arid Lands Report* in 1878.

In addition to challenging such myths as the rain-follows-the-plow theory (some scientists and booster types erroneously believed that tilling the soil enhanced and increased rainfall in an area), the *Arid Lands Report* proposed a radically different set of laws for settling the arid West. As I will discuss in a later section of this book, the *Arid Lands Report* monograph would form the basis of Powell's Irrigation Survey in the late 1880s. Yet it ultimately would be ignored until the twentieth century, long after much environmental damage had occurred in the West. Nevertheless, it marked Powell's entrance into the crusade for agricultural reform.

At this time Powell also took up the fight to consolidate the four western surveys. Besides the King Survey, which by 1878 had already finished its work along the 40th parallel, there was Lt. George Wheeler's "United States Geological Surveys West of the One Hundredth Meridian," Ferdinand V. Hayden's "United States Geological Survey of the Territories," and, of course, the Powell Survey.[30] Sometimes the surveys had met in the field and overlapped each other. As one might suspect, jealousy and turf-fighting prevailed. Consolidation, thus, seemed inevitable. That process began when New York senator Abram Hewitt slipped the consolidation into a Sundry Civil Expenses Bill in the last-minute rush at the end of a session. Even though recommended by the National Academy of Sciences, Powell's *Arid Lands Report* did not make it into the consolidation bill. The Powell Survey, however, eventually became the Smithsonian's Bureau of Ethnology with Powell as the bureau's director. Hayden lost out to Clarence King for the directorship of the combined surveys, a loss which angered Hayden and his paleontologist, Edward Cope.[31] Although he worked behind the scenes, Powell was the man who made the consolidation come into being.

Clarence King lasted all of a year and a few months as director of the newly established U.S. Geological Survey (USGS). When he quit the survey in March 1881 after a five-month leave of absence, then-President Garfield immediately named Powell to replace him. The self-taught farm youth who had learned about rocks and Indians from another self-taught scholar now headed two government bureaus specifically established to support two growing branches of science. In reality Powell had founded them both. As the two scientific disciplines outside of biology most affected by the Darwinian revolution, anthropology and geology in America had a very capable Darwinian overseeing them. What concerns us now is how he ran the USGS and how he administered public lands. Both endeavors brought him considerable praise, yet both would eventually provide enough ammunition for his enemies' cannons to blast him out of the water.

Powell clearly possessed a genius for organization. Both his supporters and critics commented on his remarkable powers of classification and synthesis. As we saw in his studies of canyon country geology, he quickly grasped and sketched the whole picture that his colleagues Dutton and Gilbert painted in. Powell ran the USGS the same way. He chose very capable assistants, shared everything he knew with them, then let them work independently. In front of congressional committees, he organized his facts and presented them clearly so that even the most unlearned congressman could understand them. According to Davis, when he appeared before legislators with his charts and maps, "he had so full command of all pertinent facts that his opponents in Congressional committees were often left with nothing but their opposition to stand on."[32]

Between 1881 and 1894 Powell built the USGS into the pride of American science. It was the largest scientific organization of its kind in the world, and the world took notice. American and European universities bestowed on Powell honorary degrees and other awards. Moreover, during his tenure the USGS budget grew from a $100,000 appropriation to as much as $719,000. Most important, however, were the number and quality of the survey's publications during Powell's years. One need only turn to any American geology bibliography today to find a number of works from Powell's men written between 1881 and 1894.

When Powell became the USGS director, his primary goal was to produce a complete topographical map of the United States.

Interestingly, his exploration of the last blank spot on the map of his country led him to initiate and oversee a plan to map that country. But he faced numerous obstacles. His first was to formulate a system of mapping conventions—symbols, colors for different rock ages, nomenclature, and so on. No uniform system existed in America or Europe, so in 1881 Powell pushed through a system that has become the American standard and has influenced European standards as well.

Another more formidable obstacle stood in his path. He needed congressional approval to map, and Powell was equal to the challenge. In 1882 he asked a friend on the House Appropriations Committee to add this phrase to the Geological Survey Sundry Civil Bill: "to continue the preparation of a geological map of the United States." Powell also solidified the survey's independence by obtaining from Interior Secretary Carl Schurz authorization to be special disbursing agent for the survey. This gave him complete freedom to allocate survey funds as he pleased.

This unprecedented power was good news and bad news. Like any successful person in the nation's capital, he quickly attracted enemies. F. V. Hayden and Edward Cope remembered their snubbing when the USGS was formed in 1879. In the mid-1880s they publicly charged that Powell's federal science programs hindered private research. Powell put this controversy to bed just as an opportunity arose to implement many of the land reform policies he had first proposed in 1878 with the *Arid Lands Report*. For almost a decade westerners had been clamoring, first separately, then collectively, for some sort of federal help with irrigation. The winter of 1886–1887 brought incredibly cold temperatures and blizzards, but a series of summer droughts followed. The western cattle boom went bust, and all the inadequacies of existing land laws revealed themselves. The rain-follows-the-plow theory blew away like tumbleweeds. Powell saw his chance.

Western congressmen, led by Nevada senator William M. Stewart, pushed for legislation in 1888 to inaugurate an irrigation survey. Powell proved the most knowledgeable and best situated man to do the job, so the Irrigation Survey fell into his lap. Or perhaps it would be better to say that he corralled it. Either way, once Powell obtained his funding—again through the indirect method of a rider to a Sundry Appropriations Bill—he sent Clarence Dutton to New Mexico where he began a school for training hydraulic engineers; A. H. Thompson continued to oversee topographic work, but his mission now focused on locating potential dam sites in the arid lands.[33] In the fall of 1888 it appeared that John Wesley Powell stood on the threshold of revolutionizing western American land law and agriculture.

The following summer Stewart and his Irrigation Committee toured the West talking to local governments and farmers about what the Irrigation Survey proposed to do. Powell caught up with the group late in the summer, and it quickly became apparent to both the Nevada senator and the Major that they harbored different visions for the Irrigation Survey. Stewart saw the survey locating dam sites and irrigable lands, then turning them over to private enterprise. He wanted laissez-faire capitalism to continue as it had in the West—with a little boost from the government. Powell's proposal bordered on socialism: cooperative control of irrigation by those within a particular watershed, and government supervision over land and water monopolies. The two ideologies clashed, and by the fall of 1889 these two men had become political enemies.

Even as Powell's men located dam sites in Utah, California, and Texas in the summer of 1889, other problems arose. Part of the original legislation for the Irrigation Survey allowed President Cleveland to withdraw all public lands from sale until the survey finished its work. This mandate protected potential dam sites and prevented speculators from following Powell's men and buying up lands identified as "irrigable." So far so good, but Powell may have pushed his luck too far in telling Congress that a complete map of the arid West should precede the sale of any more public lands. Powell's enemies insisted that such a policy might tie up the federal lands for years and that it gave Powell far too much power.

At the same time, moreover, his old enemy Cope rose up once again to attack the Major. He claimed that Powell had granted special favors to O. C. Marsh, Cope's rival and enemy; that Powell plagiarized state geological surveys; and that Powell misused USGS funds. Powell and Marsh defended themselves fairly well, but the timing for such accusations was bad.

Amid the Cope charges and the murmuring among his congressional enemies, Powell appeared before the House Appropriations Committee in June 1890. Stewart and others were waiting in
ambush. They accused Powell of misusing Irrigation Survey funds
for topographical work. They claimed that the Major was ignor-
ing artesian wells as a viable irrigation source. And they charged
that Powell encouraged government interference in America's free-
enterprise system. Powell countered with the facts, but facts often
fall short in the face of bombast and myth. The Senate reduced his
$720,000 appropriation request to $162,500.[34] With that, the Irrigation Survey died, and so did Powell's dreams of reforming western
American agriculture through scientific planning.

Powell had argued for this: Since water scarcity would allow for
only three percent of the arid West ever to be irrigated, the development of Western water resources should involve the cooperative
efforts of the federal government and local capital. The government
would locate the dam sites, then local cooperative associations, in
what he called hydrographic basins, would band together to provide
the capital, labor, and rules for establishing and distributing water.
Powell modeled these ideas on the Mormon irrigation system in
Utah as well as on other irrigation experiments in California, Colorado, and New Mexico.[35]

Powell's plan called for the sort of communal, idealistic effort
that fueled such Utopian colonies as the Mormon state of Deseret.
It combined Jeffersonian agrarianism, communalism, and American know-how. In keeping with the spirit of the times, it was opti-
mistic and progressive; it also bordered on socialistic. As such, it
butted heads with the dominant ideology of the American free-
enterprise system and the national myth of rugged individualism. Where Powell argued for limited and shared resources, the
Stewart group believed that only government interference limited
resource development.

Some have argued in retrospect that Powell's plan was imprac-
tical because it required that settlers reach a consensus as the Mormons did.[36] Either Powell was a walking anachronism whose vision
faded the way Plimoth Plantation, Brook Farm, and other utopian
communities had, or he was a prophet whose time had not yet come.
Either way, Powell's ideas of federal science eventually helped nudge

the nation toward some of the federal land policies that came of age during the Depression. Powell might not have recognized the New Deal as one of his children, but he clearly fathered some of the ideas that moved the American government, especially with regard to natural resources, toward a utopian ideal of the commons.

But in 1890 his grand plan stood defeated, and Powell decided to resign as soon as he could groom a successor. In 1894, his house in order, Powell chose Charles D. Walcott, a long-time associate from the early days of the USGS, to succeed him. Within a week of resigning, Powell checked into Johns Hopkins University Hospital where Dr. William Halstead removed several large nerves that had regenerated in Powell's stump. The Major finally gained relief from pain that had plagued him for years.[37]

When he returned to Washington after the operation, he moved all his belongs to the Bureau of Ethnology in the Adams Building. There he revised *Exploration* for republication by a private press. Flood and Vincent of Chautauqua Press published *Canyons of the Colorado* in 1895. An enlarged edition of the 1875 government publication, it served as a coffee-table version of Powell's adventure story. It did not achieve the substantial sales that the author and publisher had dreamed of.[38]

Powell also wrote three essays for *National Geographic* and other publications, but this ethnologist's real interest lay in formulating and putting to paper a survey of "man's knowledge and philosophy through the span of time from the primitive savage ... to the modern age of science and technology."[39] That effort, *Truth and Error*, appeared in 1898. The first volume of a never-completed trilogy, this strange book attempted to be an introduction to the philosophy of science. Reviewers did not line up to praise the book, nor has anyone since. Undaunted, Powell pushed on with the second part of the trilogy, *Good and Evil*, published posthumously. The projected third part of the trilogy, *Pleasure and Pain*, never progressed further than the few essays.

In the years between his resignation from the USGS in 1894 and his death in 1902, Powell spent increasingly less time running the Bureau of Ethnology. He had largely turned over the bureau to W. J. McGee. Besides working on his philosophical/ethnographic writings during this time, he purchased a house in Brooklin, Maine, in

1896 and spent long summers there sailing and studying the local Penobscot Indians. In November of 1901, increasingly frail and in bad health, Powell suffered a stroke. He recovered by the New Year, but the next summer in Maine suffered another. He died there on 23 September 1902 at the age of sixty-eight.

2 Interpreting Powell's Writings on Exploration, Land Planning, and Anthropology

Laypersons reading Powell's account of the 1869 trip down the Colorado River might not stop to consider that more than one version of the story exists, or they might not bother to see which texts they were reading. In fact, four published versions of the story appeared in Powell's lifetime, although only two accounts circulate today. Moreover, some of the material and illustrations differ greatly from one version to the next.

The text that Powell scholars usually refer to has one of those laborious and lengthy titles typical of Victorian scientific publications—*Exploration of the Colorado River of the West and Its Tributaries. Explored in 1869, 1870, 1871, and 1872 Under the Direction of the Secretary of the Smithsonian Institution.* The book is divided into two parts, with both parts subdivided into sections. Part one contains an account of three "original explorations." We will focus on the first of two of those "explorations," both of which were written by Powell and carry the title, "The History of the Exploration of the Canyons of the Colorado." (Section three was written by A. H. Thompson.)

Section one recounts in eight chapters the 1869 trip from Green River, Wyoming, on 24 May to the mouth of the Virgin River on

1 September. Section two, chapter nine, narrates an 1870 journey through present-day Zion National Park across the Arizona Strip to the Uinkaret Plateau. This trip culminated in Powell meeting and talking to the Shivwits Paiute Indians who reportedly murdered his three men the year before. Part two is a serious geological treatise on the canyon country entitled "On the Physical Features of the Valley of the Colorado." As with section three of part one, we will ignore part two.

Even though this 1875 version of the Powell expedition is the official one and predominates in Powell studies, one published account predated it. Another came out simultaneously, and a fourth appeared twenty years later. The first, "Major J. W. Powell's Report on His Exploration of the Rio Colorado in 1869," appeared in 1870 in W. A. Bell's second edition of *New Tracks in America*. The simultaneous version was a three-part series of articles for *Scribner's Magazine* entitled "Canyons of the Colorado," with a fourth article, "An Overland Trip to the Grand Canyon," tacked on. Behind those texts lie at least two journals, numerous newspaper reports, and many oral presentations by Powell in the years between 1869 and 1874, when he completed *Exploration*. The fourth version was the 1895 *Canyons of the Colorado*, published by Flood and Vincent of Chautauqua Press.

It appears that all along Powell imagined a popular account of the trip. But in order to ensure future funding, Spencer Baird and Representative Garfield urged the Major to hurry and complete his report, detailing for Congress his exploration of the canyons. So in the spring of 1874 Powell sat down, finished his manuscript—the sections on exploration and the geological treatise—and submitted it for government publication.

By this time Powell had hired a secretary, James C. Pilling, who served as an amanuensis. No doubt Powell composed *Exploration* by dictating to Pilling. Years later, after Powell's death, Grove Karl Gilbert explained Powell's method of composition, saying that the Major generally worked without notes and either paced as he dictated or sat swiveling in his chair, "raising his voice and gesturing with hand and body as though addressing an audience."[1]

Gilbert also contends that Powell always thought out and organized his subject before he dictated. Thus, when he finally spoke to his amanuensis, Powell could pay close attention "to the selection of words and phrases and the framing of sentences."[2] Gillbert maintains that, unlike most nineteenth-century writers who wrote long, effusive sentences, Powell developed a concise, short-sentence style precisely because he thought out his subject in advance. After composition, Powell usually circulated his manuscript among colleagues to solicit criticism.[3] Gilbert's comments on Powell's style as terse and imagistic help explain what makes *Exploration* such riveting reading. Powell's concise, journalistic prose perfectly matched his action-filled adventure story. Moreover, he summoned his refined visual sense many times to describe the canyon country.

In analyzing chapters one through nine of *Exploration*, we must acknowledge that Powell took historical liberties with some facts in order to shape his story. For example, he selected numerous incidents from later expeditions, including names given, and placed them in the 1869 story. Glen Canyon, for instance, received its name after the 1871–1872 expedition. It originally boasted two names: Mound Canyon, from the Dirty Devil to the San Juan; and Monument Canyon, from the San Juan to the Paria. Another transposition of events involves the first part of chapter nine. Powell recounts an 1872 exploration of Parunuweap Canyon in present-day Zion National Park as happening in 1870. Apparently he did so because this was one of the "original explorations" he refers to his "Preface" and because it fit sequentially and geographically with his Uinkaret Plateau trip to discover the fate of his three murdered crew members.[4]

Colorado River historians like Stanton, Stone, and Marston criticized Powell for transposing facts. In some ways they made a good case against Powell. After all, *Exploration* was conducted under the government's auspices. Powell's defense, if he wanted to make it, could only be literary. Moreover, Powell stated that he would only write about the "original explorations" (his reason for not talking about the 1871–1872 trip). So he faced two problems: how to include information like names given at a later date, and at the same time make his narrative hold together. Had he merely put events in sequential order, the end product would have been much less readable and inclusive. As the next section will show, Powell opted for art over exact chronology, even though he never distorted any scientific fact.

This dilemma of science versus art has received attention from the noted Western historian William Goetzmann, in his *The West of the Imagination*. Although he discusses the problem of the scientific artist in the West, Goetzmann's comments apply equally well to literary scientists like Powell, King, and Dutton. He says that while survey painters always tried for scientific objectivity and representation, the "artist's feeling of awe or wonder at the moment of viewing inevitably allowed his emotions to give form and character to the pictures."[5] Likewise for writers. Not only did Powell and others bring with them prevailing associations and impressions of Romanticism, but the landscape itself moved them to excess. Despite a desire to portray things with scientific accuracy and detachment, Powell sometimes could not help himself. As he said in the conclusion to *Canyons of the Colorado*, "The wonders of the Grand Canyon cannot be adequately represented in symbols of speech, nor by speech itself. The resources of the graphic art are taxed beyond their powers in attempting to portray its features. Language and illustration combined must fail."[6] While scientist Powell sought facts over myth, writer Powell of Victorian America was helping to create and perpetuate certain other myths about the American West.

In the opening chapter of *Exploration* (which contains the subheading "Canyon Myth"), Powell recalls some of the wild and wonderful myths that "prevented the traveler from penetrating the country, so that, until the Colorado River Exploring Expedition was organized, it was unknown."[7] Myth said the Colorado River sucked boats down into whirlpools never to be seen again, that the river disappeared underground for long stretches, and that it possessed great waterfalls. In addition to these tall tales about the river, Powell also retells a Paiute myth on the origins of the Grand Canyon. The story's moral says that one enters the canyon in defiance of the gods who created it. Powell proceeds to ignore the Indian myths as well as others in order to make "some geological studies."[8]

Thus, the man who later became the "High Priest of American Science" replaced the Indian gods with the god of Science. And this heroic pursuit of Science, this unraveling of the unknown, becomes the major theme and provides the basic structure of the story. Powell employs the archetypal hero/quest motif to frame his narrative. This is not to say that Powell consciously decided to use what John Cawelti calls the simplest and oldest in appeal of all story types.⁹ Rather, he hardly could have told his story any other way. After all, he was exploring the last blank spot on the U.S. map. And one senses from Powell's narrative that this spot, the Colorado River country, remained blank for so long because of its difficulty to penetrate and also because it contained some of the world's deepest scientific secrets.

Many students of myth have talked about the hero quest, but none better than Joseph Campbell in *The Hero with a Thousand Faces*. Campbell's definition of the hero quest perfectly describes the basic structure of Powell's story: "A hero ventures forth from the world of common day into a region of supernatural wonder; fabulous forces are there encountered and a decisive victory is won: the hero comes back from this mysterious adventure with the power to bestow boons on his fellow man."¹⁰ Powell is the scientist/hero who enters the fabled canyon country to roll back the myths, to reveal the secrets of the rocks, and thus to unravel the mysteries of Earth's origins. Although he achieves a victory, it comes at a high price— three men dead who ignored the calculations of the scientist/hero. Another feature of adventure stories, John Cawelti says, is that the hero figure usually displays exceptional strength, though he is sometimes marked by a flaw.¹¹ Powell, the one-armed veteran of Shiloh, falls into this category. Numerous times throughout the narrative, while he is climbing a cliff or being thrown into a churning rapid, his maimed arm nearly hastens his death.

Powell's "call to adventure," as Campbell puts it, revolves around the canyon country being the last unexplored spot in the United States. Near the end of the Separation Rapid story, when Powell faces mutiny by three crew members, he almost decides to leave the river. But then he remembers what brought him there, saying that "for years I have been contemplating this trip. To leave the exploration unfinished, to say that there is a part of the canyon which I cannot explore, having almost accomplished it, is more than I am willing to acknowledge."¹² Clearly Powell felt destined to explore the canyon country, and that conviction helped him face the greatest trial of a very difficult trip.

Most quest stories contain guide figures, and so does this one. But the guide here differs from Dante's Virgil or James Fenimore Cooper's Indian scout, Chingachgook. As befits his scientific quest, Powell is guided by his scientific instruments—his barometer, his sextant, and his thermometer. Throughout the trip he determines his location by using these instruments. Their significance becomes most apparent at the expedition's first crisis, Disaster Falls. When Powell thinks they have lost the instruments, he decides to halt the expedition to replace them. Fortunately, his men recover them downstream. Later, a certain jealousy attaches to those instruments. Numerous times the men complain about Powell's stopping to geologize or map the country, especially when supplies dwindle in the Grand Canyon. These particular feelings bubble over when the party reaches Separation Rapid and Powell brings out the sextant to determine their location. Those who follow the guidance of the scientific instruments are saved while those who do not, perish.

Campbell speaks of the hero being swallowed into the "belly of the whale" where he "may be said to have died to time and returned to the World Womb, the World Navel."[13] This element figures strongly in Powell's narrative. Each canyon the crew enters is spoken of as a further penetration into the unknown. Many of the names they give the canyons—"Lodore" (from Robert Southey's poem), "Desolation," "Labyrinth," and "Marble"—suggest they are traveling through a mysterious, otherworldly landscape. And with each new canyon, they come closer and closer to the "belly of the whale," the axis mundi. That, of course, is the Grand Canyon itself, from the Little Colorado River to the Grand Wash Cliffs.

In his famous 13 August passage about entering "the Great Unknown," Powell's language expresses at once both fear and audacity before the gods. He mentions the nearly exhausted food supplies and "the fretful river." To emphasize the magnitude of this unknown, he describes their location as being "three quarters of a mile in the depths of the earth" where "the great river shrinks into insignificance." He calls the waves "angry" as they dash "against the walls and cliffs that rise to the world above," and his men "but pygmies, running up and down the sands, or lost among the boulders."[14] The language implies that Powell, like Odysseus and Aeneas before him, has entered an underworld of sorts where he, Science, and his guiding instruments will be tested.

Telling this story after the event, Powell also played off the numerous reports of his death while on the river. From the beginning of the journey, charlatans and publicity-seekers like John Risdon claimed knowledge of the Powell party's demise. These rumors appeared in newspapers from Utah to New York. Powell even mentions the public's fascination with his imminent death. After he exits the Grand Canyon and meets with the Mormon bishop, Mr. Leithead, he writes that "some weeks before, a messenger had been sent from Salt Lake City, with instructions for them to watch for any fragments or relics of our party that might drift down the stream."[15] The Mormon hierarchy, and probably the rest of the nation, presumed that Powell and his crew had died somewhere in the canyons. This anecdote reinforces the theme of symbolic death-to-time that Powell may be said to have experienced.

Like most quest stories, this one involves a series of initiations in which the hero must submit to and merge with the opposing forces. The crisis at Disaster Falls and Powell's near fall at Echo Park (this actually happened in Desolation Canyon) both test the hero's mettle and teach him about the canyon's power. But the ultimate test, as mentioned before, comes at Separation Rapid. Everything that had guided the hero up to then is on the line. In order to dissuade the mutineers, the scientist/hero reads the stars with his sextant. At Disaster Falls the Howlands had not followed Powell's signals to pull over; now they are once again questioning the scientist's authority. Along with William Dunn, they reject Science and walk to their deaths on the Shivwits Plateau. The other men, however, stand by the scientist/hero who leads them to safety, out of the belly of the whale.

The final section of the story, chapter nine, forms an epilogue to the Separation incident. The overland trip to the Uinkaret Plateau (east of the Shivwits) seeks to clean up the mystery of the three mutineers' deaths, but first Powell persuades his Paiute guides to tell him a few of their stories. The one he recounts here loosely parallels Powell's own reasons for traveling to meet the Shivwits. Their story relates how So'-Kus Wai-un-ats, or One-Two Boys, avenged his father's death. Like One-Two Boys, Powell is seeking to learn of the death of loved ones. But in this case the roles are reversed. Powell, the father figure, seeks to unravel the mystery of his three prodigal sons' deaths. Also in keeping with his original intention to use science to undo the Indian myths of the canyons, Powell's journey ends in peace rather than in the violence of the Paiute myth. One-Two Boys kills Stone Shirt, the man who killed his father and stole his mother. But Powell, the scientist, makes a pow-wow with the Shivwits, passes the peace pipe with them, and listens as they tell how they mistook Powell's men for the murderers of a Hualapai woman from south of the river.

Powell gains the Shivwits' trust by speaking their language. He writes: "I do not wish to trade, do not want their lands.... I tell them I wish to learn about their canyons and mountains, and about themselves."[16] In going to meet the Shivwits, once again Powell is traveling into an unknown, this time an ethnographic one. The Shivwits Paiutes were some of the last North American Indians that whites contacted. Powell describes them as "more nearly in their primitive condition than any others on the continent. They have never received anything from the Government, and are too poor to tempt the trader, and their country is so nearly inaccessible that the white man never visits them."[17] There is a sense that seeing the Shivwits will reveal to the ethnographer how people lived at the dawn of creation.

With this trip's completion, the last blank spot on the map and the last "wild" tribe of Indians had been snatched from the misty regions of myth and placed on the shelf with the other great discoveries of Science. The hero has completed his task and returned to tell the nation of his feats. Campbell says that questing heroes "come to the knowledge of this unity in multiplicity."[18] That had been Powell's intent in stripping the map's blank spot of its myth and laying bare the scientific facts of the region's geology and ethnography. Powell's metaphors reinforce that idea, especially his use of the nature-as-book metaphor.

This trope had become a cliché by the time Powell went west to unravel the mysteries of the Grand Canyon. The metaphor's use in American scientific writing derived from the work of the esteemed Harvard scientist Louis Agassiz. An effective figure of speech, it implied first an author, an ordering hand who wrote the book, a concept that would appeal to a monotheistic, Christian culture. Second, this metaphor suggests a readable order that anyone schooled in the language can decipher. Finally, it speaks of natural history as a neat progression. That certainly would attract a classifying mind like Powell's. It would have particularly appealed to someone viewing the neatly stacked layers of sedimentary formations that one finds in the canyon country. As Powell says shortly after entering the Grand Canyon, "All about me are interesting geological records. The book is open, and I can read as I run."[19]

He uses the metaphor numerous other times, obviously thinking of the canyons in those terms from at least 1869 on. (A joking reference to the metaphor appears in Jack Summer's journal early in the trip near Kingfisher Canyon.[20]) When Powell wrote the first account of his trip for W. A. Bell's *New Tracks in America*, he gave the metaphor some moral weight by declaring that "the canyons of this region would be a book of revelations in the rock-leaved Bible of geology,"[21] suggesting that at one point Powell thought of his expedition in prophetic terms. If the canyon country is the bible of geology, as many would agree, Powell would stand as the high priest of that sacred text. When he wrote *Exploration* he dropped the biblical aspect of the metaphor. Perhaps his editors thought it sacrilegious. If so, that is not the only problem with the metaphor.

To speak of nature as a book says that the natural order is fixed— sitting there like so many pages bound and set for all time. To anti-evolutionists like Agassiz this metaphor perfectly described nature. But for Darwinists like Powell it should have created problems. He saw the canyon country as the creation of powerful geological forces; these forces of erosion, wind, and uplift, moreover, were still carving the canyon. If this is true—and subsequent study has done everything to confirm Powell's initial theory—then the book that he read in 1869 would not be the same one if read years later.

John Muir solved this problem by abandoning the book metaphor for the palimpsest metaphor.[22] A palimpsest is a document that has been written over numerous times. This metaphor better suggests an evolving, changing landscape, though for some reason Powell ignored this clearer figure of speech. He probably used the former because nineteenth-century readers found it so accessible. And this part of Powell's account was written largely for the middle-class readers of *Scribner's* as well as for congressmen.

Like the book metaphor, Powell's other dominant metaphors derive from familiar nineteenth-century stock. Wallace Stegner says that every western report from Lewis and Clark onward used architectural terms to describe the rock outcroppings they found in the West. Powell was no exception. Stegner goes on to say that the parallel "was no mere suggestion, but a 'vivid resemblance' ... revealed not occasionally but everywhere."[23]

Paul Shepard in *Man in the Landscape* goes a few steps further than Stegner and offers a provocative explanation for this phenomenon. "Rocks of certain angular shapes," he theorizes, "may always mean 'man-made structure' to European-Americans because of an indelible association of form with human works perceived at a crucial moment in mental development."[24] He likens this cultural phenomenon to "the biological syndrome associated with 'imprinting.'"[25] If accurate, Powell could hardly have helped himself in using this metaphor. At one point, however, he recognizes its limitations. When he enters Marble Canyon and describes its great limestone alcoves, he writes that, a "great number of caves are hollowed out, and carvings seen, which suggest architectural forms, though on a scale so grand that architectural terms belittle them."[26] Still, he seems not to know what to use instead.

Powell's other figures of speech come largely from the pool of nineteenth-century romanticism. Numerous times he refers to clouds as children playing in the canyons. Romanticism espoused the cult of the child as a symbol of pure innocence. Also, many of the names Powell stuck on canyon features come right out of the romantic school of the sublime: "Music Temple," "Cliff of the Harp," "Marble Canyon," and "Hell's Half Mile" exemplify a few of the names reflecting romanticism's penchant for emotion and the exotic. Although the details and the methodology of *Exploration* reflect the literary movement of realism, the ideas, themes, and images of this book clearly harken back to romanticism. This is not surprising since Powell's life bridged the two literary periods.

Little changed when *Canyons of the Colorado* appeared after Powell retired from the USGS in 1894. The book apparently was published to meet a growing public demand for reissuance of the long-out-of-print *Exploration*. This final version of Powell's river trip and overland explorations proved to be a good summation of his entire career as explorer, physiographer, ethnographer, and geologist.

The text for the 1869 river trip and the overland trip to the Uinkaret Plateau in *Canyons of the Colorado* is virtually identical to that of *Exploration*, at least in chapters one through nine. The only differences involve eliminating some punctuation, joining some sentences, and changing a few words. But Powell added considerable written and illustrative material to *Canyons*. And even though he included the 1876 *Scribner's* article, "The Ancient Province of Tusayan," it bears only a broad resemblance to the magazine article. The Chautauqua Press version supplies considerably more ethnographic information on—and many images of—Hopis and other Southwest Indians, reflecting nearly two decades of serious ethnographic work by Powell and his Bureau of Ethnology. "The impression he leaves," says Powell biographer Donald Worster, "is of a land densely populated by Indians, not a wilderness but a fully settled and inhabited place. . . . he was suggesting. . . the peoples living in this environment must be studied and appreciated along with the facts of geology or the sublime color and spaciousness of nature. . . . A science that leaves the native people out is partial and inadequate."[27]

In this popular book, Powell dropped the geological treatise that formed part two of *Exploration*. Instead, he opened the book with a ninety-page overview of Colorado Basin physiography and ethnology. Written for the layperson, this still constitutes one of the most comprehensive and illuminating descriptions of Colorado Plateau environmental history. Although much read today by the general reader, this overview has somehow escaped the notice of current environmental historians. Considering the attention these historians give Powell's work and ideas, one can only wonder why.

Canyons of the Colorado also greatly expanded the number of illustrations found in the earlier volume. Powell used over 250 of them from virtually every Powell Survey, USGS, and Bureau of Ethnology publication pertaining to the Colorado Plateau. Although these illustrations surpass those of *Exploration* in quality, sometimes they bear no relation to the text. No doubt this glut of illustrations proved popular with turn-of-the-century audiences, just as it does today.

Finally, Powell added a ten-page conclusion, "The Grand Canyon," to *Canyons of the Colorado*. Appropriately placed since the Grand Canyon is the geologic and aesthetic crescendo of the Colorado Plateau, this piece describes how emotions wash over the canyon watcher—a perfect way to end this popular edition of his work. It is as concise a statement of Powell's feelings for landscape as any critic will ever find.

All in all, *Canyons of the Colorado* is a distinctly different book from *Exploration*. Although some have admonished Powell for publishing for profit, this book added much new material and presented in a very accessible way more than twenty years of scientific work on the Colorado Plateau. The book's organization holds together quite well. Moreover, compared with *Exploration*, *Canyons of the Colorado* paints a more complete picture of the Colorado Plateau and the Major's work there. It is to another aspect of Powell's work—land policy and reclamation—that we now turn our attention.

While Powell's interest in agriculture stemmed from his own farming experiences, his concern for western agriculture and irrigation began on his first visits to Colorado in 1867 and 1868. But it is difficult to say exactly when Powell first thought of writing something like the *Arid Lands Report*. Powell biographer William Culp Darrah states that Powell began composing it in 1874, simultaneously with *Exploration* and *Geology of the Eastern Uinta Mountains*. After these works were published in 1875 and 1876, respectively, Powell quickly pulled together the *Arid Lands Report* manuscript and on 1 April 1878 submitted it to Land Office chief, J. A. Williamson. As we saw, he wanted it included in the legislation consolidating the four surveys.

Powell wrote most of the sections of this report, although his colleagues, Grove Karl Gilbert, Clarence E. Dutton, and Almon H. Thompson, assisted with chapters of their own. Their sections, however, reflect their chief's ideas, so one can say unequivocally that this is Powell's book.

Taking up the question of public lands in the arid region—those east of the Sierra Nevada ranges and west of the hundredth meridian—the *Arid Lands Report* offers as radical a critique of the laws, institutions, and myths of western lands as nineteenth-century America ever saw. It questioned the Homestead Act, a well-meaning land law that proved mostly useless in the West. It questioned the capitalistic practices of land and water speculation and urged a more socialistic system of apportionment. It questioned the applicability of Anglo-Saxon riparian water law in an arid region. It questioned various pseudoscientific ideas like the rain-follows-the-plow theory. It questioned the myth of the West as a garden, a myth that had been propounded by railroads, speculators, and western congressmen. And finally, it questioned our national myths of rugged individualism and self-reliance, as well as the belief that it is an American birthright to acquire enormous wealth. In short, Powell wanted to remake America in the West.

As one can imagine, when Powell's report appeared as H.R. Executive Document 73, many congressmen and western newspapers decried it as socialistic, or worse. Most probably did not even read it. As with many controversial books like *Origin of the Species* or Salman Rushdie's *Satanic Verses*, most people learned about Powell's ideas by hearsay. Those who suspected their pocketbooks might suffer or their fundamental beliefs be overturned by reason and facts rose up, thumped their chests in self-righteous indignation, and said "no."

If most congressmen and farmers had read this report, they would have found this: while the Homestead Act gave 160 acres to anyone who could "prove up" on the land by building a house and living there, in practice the act led to widespread land fraud. Only a tiny fraction of western land actually had enough water on it to support a family farm. Many families, thus, lost their claims and returned east. Others who held onto their land often did so by deceit, in the process sometimes acquiring numerous sections.

Powell proposed that only eighty acres of irrigated land be given to any individual. But he also wanted lands suitable for irrigation to become part of an irrigation district. Such districts would be established by no fewer than nine persons who would write their own laws regarding the water. District members would also provide the labor and capital for the irrigation works. Powell believed that the "association of a number of people prevents single individuals from having undue control of natural privileges."[28] He called this the "colony system" and based it on the thirty-year Mormon experiment in Utah. Powell believed in the little man and knew that, especially in the arid region, little men acquired strength in numbers and through cooperation.

Like Powell's farmer, his rancher would also participate in a colony system of shared pastures. But Powell saw that those lands deemed suitable for grazing rather than farming must substantially exceed the 160-acre limit of the Homestead Act. Scant vegetation dictated that no less than 2,560 acres would support a ranching family. Even then, that family would need some irrigation water for gardens and the like. Again, in his plans for ranchers Powell would not grant tracts to individuals, but to groups of nine persons forming a grazing district. This district would share an open range of common pastures. Thus, a group of nine persons would work 23,040 acres.

An essential principle underlying Powell's irrigation and grazing districts was this: the lay of the land should dictate land use and land distribution. In the humid East an imposed rectangular grid plan had proved a fairly reasonable and equitable way of parceling land. In the West, Powell knew that aridity dictated a different set of conditions by which land planners ought to abide. In other words, Powell was saying that a thousand years or so of European, wetlands agricultural ideas and parceling systems could not work in the arid region. He wanted the nation to change its agricultural paradigm and, accordingly, its laws and institutions. This was a tall order for a young country bent on rapid expansion.

But Powell, never timid, went further with his radical recommendations. He wanted to change the centuries-old system of water appropriation. Under English Common Law, England and then America developed a system of water law where water was nearly as common as air. This "riparian rights" system gave anyone owning a bank of a stream the right to use that water, provided he returned it to the stream. For example, in Middlesex or Kentucky one might use water to run a mill, but one would not need to irrigate in those places. In the arid region, irrigation proves very necessary, but returning that water to the stream afterwards is nearly impossible. Thus, today, downstream users like Mexico at the tail end of the Colorado Basin often see nothing but a dry riverbed. Powell wanted to tie water rights to the land and determine just how much water each parcel would need and could obtain. That way, no one would buy land without water.

Although flawed in some respects by today's standards, the *Arid Lands Report* saw far ahead of its time. As such it proved too spicy a dish for Congress, even though the National Academy of Sciences wholeheartedly supported it. Powell was poking too many sacred cows and exploding too many popular myths. He was calling for restraint and limited settlement in a country that perceived its continent's resources as unlimited. He was also questioning certain aspects of our economic system. While he never actually called capitalism an evil, exploitive system, he railed against its excesses: monopolies and land and water speculation. Moreover, Powell was asking the country's land planners to abandon their geometric thinking and conceive of land units based on natural systems like water basins.

While Powell pointed out many of the shortcomings of American cultural paradigms, hindsight shows that his plans for a communally settled, arid land paradise contained flaws. For example, even though Powell and Gilbert noted surface water increase in Utah since settlement in 1847, they did not connect that increase to watershed degradation. In fact, altering the vegetation in the arid region led to drastic consequences for water conservation and wildlife habitat.

A second flaw in this report centers on Powell's plan to remove Indians, and hence fire, he thought, from the forests. Although a decade later Powell was beginning to understand fire's role in forest ecology, in 1878 he merely saw fire as something that destroyed lumber resources. In addition, for someone who called himself an ethnologist, he somehow ignored the importance of forest hunting to certain tribes. But then Powell also expected Indians to join in his agrarian commonwealth; the pursuit of game, Indian fashion, did not appear in that picture.

A third flaw that some critics have discussed is the practical feasibility of Powell's colony system. Historian Thomas Alexander has criticized Powell's plan as anachronistic and unrealistic.[29] Finally, perhaps the greatest flaw of the report, from an ecological point of view, was that the Major's purpose was strictly utilitarian. His goal was maximum efficiency, the greatest good for the greatest number of people. While Powell certainly looked further ahead than most of his contemporaries, he did not look as far as a Henry Thoreau or a John Muir when it came to national ecologic health.

Whatever one might say about Powell's vision or blindness in the *Arid Lands Report,* it remains a singularly important contribution to American land policy. Many of its ideas ultimately found form in the various laws and government agencies established to protect grazing (the Bureau of Land Management), water (the Bureau of Reclamation), and timber (the U.S. Forest Service). It also laid the foundation for Theodore Roosevelt's and Gifford Pinchot's sweeping Progressive conservation reforms in the early 1900s, and it inspired the New Deal's Soil and Water Conservation Districts. For better or worse, it has been called the first environmental impact statement. It certainly speaks to our own age, even if it could not make itself heard above the roar of its own times.

The founding of the Bureau of American Ethnology (originally the Bureau of Ethnology) in 1879, and Powell's subsequent direction of that bureau until his death in 1902, was, as Wallace Stegner puts it, "one of the two great works of his life."[30] Powell's genius for organization and delegation expressed itself most clearly in anthropology. When Powell began practicing anthropology it was a nascent science, full of amateurs and wild theories. When he left it, his bureau had stamped the seal of "serious science" on the discipline. While many of Powell's own anthropological theories have been discarded, the bureau he founded, like the USGS, became one of the foremost scientific organizations in the world. It remains so today.

As we noted, Powell's interest in Native Americans grew out of his childhood digs with George Crookham and his teenage encounters with Winnebago Indians camped on the family farm in Wisconsin. His professional work began in 1868 at Meeker Bottoms, Colorado. The discipline of anthropology that Powell began practicing that winter may have lacked a long professional tradition, but it did not lack a strong conceptual background. Powell understood his intellectual legacy: namely, the Enlightenment and the contemporaneous work of Charles Darwin, Thomas Malthus, Herbert Spencer, and Lewis Henry Morgan.

The eighteenth-century Enlightenment had introduced two very important ideas that nineteenth-century anthropologists took to heart. For one, Locke, Montesquieu, and others had preached tolerance and the importance of "comparative anthropology." This term should not be mistaken for what we today call "cultural relativism"; rather, comparative anthropology said that each culture had to be studied in its own context. But the second idea the Enlightenment bequeathed to anthropology—progress—put those cultural contexts into a "correct sequence" for civilized Europeans. In other words, belief in progress encouraged the notion of racial superiority, even among the greatest social thinkers of the day. As Marvin Harris says, by the 1860s "anthropology and racial determinism had become synonymous. The only issue was whether inferior races could improve."[31] While racism is certainly as old as humanity, Harris says, in the nineteenth century nations were for the first time rewarding their wise men for proving "that the supremacy of one people over another was the inevitable outcome of the biological laws of universe."[32] Malthus, Spencer, and Morgan, each in his own way, attempted to prove this racial doctrine. John Wesley Powell, a step behind these first-rate thinkers, did the same in his own anthropological studies. He was especially influenced by Morgan, one of the founding fathers of anthropology.

Morgan's classic study, *Ancient Society* (1877), established a theory of cultural evolution that Powell adopted for his own work. Based on his studies of Iroquois Indians, Morgan proposed an elaborate theory of human social evolution from what he called "savagery" through "barbarism" to "civilization." Each stage, divided into lower, middle, and upper, was marked by certain modes of food production and technological and cultural development. In addition to noting and describing stages, Morgan's theory preached the superiority of white Europeans and the inferiority of the so-called savage. While anthropologists today reject Morgan's theories, they accept his categories with some modifications.

Although Powell rejected his other contemporary, Herbert Spencer, and his notion of "survival of the fittest," he bought many of Morgan's ideas. Doing so may have skewed his interpretations, but following Morgan certainly helped his fieldwork. In that respect Powell made some lasting contributions. One way in which he agreed with Morgan and parted company with some other social scientists was in the question of biological differences. As Donald Worster states, "[O]n one theme Powell was always clear and emphatic. Cultural evolution had nothing to do with biological differences between humans."[33] In that respect, Powell was ahead of many of the racialist theories at the time, especially those who measured skulls to prove one race superior to another, a practice Stephen Jay Gould called the "Mismeasure of Man." Powell also believed that biological integration was inevitable.[34]

Some critics claim that Powell was not a good fieldworker. That misconception was dispelled in 1971 when Don and Catherine Fowler published a compilation of Powell's work on the Numic people in *Anthropology of the Numa: John Wesley Powell's Manuscripts on the Numic Peoples of Western North America, 1868–1880*. This collection of myths, customs, songs, vocabularies, place names, and other data comprises a substantial contribution to our understanding of the Numic peoples—the Ute, Paiute, Shoshone, and Bannock Indians of the Intermountain West. Powell's collection of stories and songs adds to and authenticates much of the material gathered by later anthropologists. Moreover, his collection of the material culture of the Numa (now deposited in the National Museum of Natural History) is one of the largest and most varied of its kind. But Powell's major contribution to Indian studies came in linguistics. The Fowlers tell us that he "collected a large corpus of linguistic data from several Numic groups."[35] Out of those investigations grew a major study classifying Indian languages, his *Introduction to the Study of Indian Languages* (1877; 2nd ed. 1880).

The larger work of the bureau produced some landmark publications in Native American studies. Besides Powell's Indian language classification, we have C. C. Royce's monumental checklist of treaties made with Indians from 1606 to 1885. Most significantly, perhaps, Powell initiated *The Handbook of American Indians* (1907). What began as a dictionary of names grew, over many years of work by various noted anthropologists, into what is still one of the most indispensable reference works on Native Americans.

When one walks into the Smithsonian's Anthropological Archives today, one sees a series of life-sized pictures of great moments and men in American anthropology. The first panel shows Major Powell standing with a Paiute leader, Tau-gu, pointing at something in the distance. Even if Franz Boas, the father of modern anthropology and cultural relativism, left Powell behind, Powell clearly led and legitimized the field of anthropology in America, pointing the way for Boas and his followers. I like to think that is what this picture says.

The West that Powell had sought to settle in a rational manner based on the conditions of the environment had, in the Turnerian terms which Powell endorsed, officially closed shortly before his death. His vision, however, did not fully guide that settlement. Much suffering and failure attended whites' settling of the West, in good part because of the myths that Powell had fought against. Nevertheless, Powell bequeathed to the nation a legacy of fearless exploration, brilliant science, and dedicated public service.

Paiute leader Tau-gu with John Wesley Powell.
Richard Wright Young Collection. Courtesy Special Collections, J. Willard Marriott Library, University of Utah.

Lining boats at Ashley Falls, Green River.
Richard Wright Young Collection. Courtesy Special Collections, J. Willard Marriott Library, University of Utah.

Sentinel Rock in Glen Canyon, along the Colorado River.
Richard Wright Young Collection. Courtesy Special Collections, J. Willard Marriott Library, University of Utah.

Marble Canyon, Colorado River, looking upstream.
Richard Wright Young Collection. Courtesy Special Collections, J. Willard Marriott Library, University of Utah.

John Wesley Powell's boat. Grand Canyon, Colorado River.
Richard Wright Young Collection. Courtesy Special Collections, J. Willard Marriott Library, University of Utah.

Vishnu Schist buttresses, Monument Creek, Colorado River, Grand Canyon.
Richard Wright Young Collection. Courtesy Special Collections, J. Willard Marriott Library, University of Utah.

Granite Rapid in Grand Canyon.
Richard Wright Young Collection. Courtesy Special Collections, J. Willard Marriott Library,
University of Utah.

3　Interpretations of Powell on Irrigation

In everyday life the average person first encounters John Wesley Powell through Lake Powell, the reservoir that backs up behind Glen Canyon Dam in northern Arizona. By naming the reservoir after Powell, the Bureau of Reclamation was stating implicitly that he would have supported the bureau's large dam-building program. Yet after people have grasped this and have made a few more trips to the lake, they usually learn that environmentalists want to decommission the dam and that the same environmentalists also believe that Powell's name has been used in vain. Environmentalists say that Powell would never have approved of such big reclamation projects as Glen Canyon Dam, Flaming Gorge Dam, or any of the scores of "cash-register dams" the bureau erected in the twentieth century.[1]

In fact, in the substantial literature about Powell written between the end of his life and the present, his name has been invoked many times to further a point of view one way or another about reclamation and irrigation. This is not surprising since no American in the late nineteenth century knew more about the broad picture of western irrigation than John Wesley Powell. As we noted earlier, as head of the United States Geological Survey in 1889 when Congress enacted the Irrigation Survey and entrusted it to his agency, Powell planned and oversaw a massive effort to map and survey the West for potential dam sites. Moreover, prior to this and consequent with it, he wrote extensively on the subject, as in the *Arid Lands Report.* Thus, on reclamation questions, having Powell on one's side would appear to give the weight of tradition. It is nice to have such an authority figure along for the ride when the ride is as wild as something like western land and water issues. For historians of the reclaimed West Powell stands not only as the source, but, as the issues have inevitably evolved, the lightning rod as well. It is no wonder the waters of reclamation history flow a bit muddy when it comes to Powell. But then, what historical waters do not?

Part of what the debate about Powell and big dams shows is the way in which historians often use presentist values to interpret the past and its major figures. Every historian tells stories and those stories are shaped by the times and by the culture. As Stephen Tatum has shown so well in his fine study of Billy the Kid's interpreters, no interpreter of the past can totally efface his own personality or devise a language untinged by personality or learned cultural traditions.[2] That certainly has been the case with John Wesley Powell and big dams in the Colorado River Basin. Particularly, would Powell have approved or opposed the reservoir named after him? The answer is not simple, but I will attempt one by the end of this section. Ultimately, however, that answer will serve a larger purpose; namely, why have historians—often contradicting one another—chosen to see Powell and the past as they have? Or to put it another way, how should we view the past and the ways in which we inevitably alter it?

Let me say at the beginning that I define "historian" broadly, that is, as anyone who writes about the past in the generally accepted way that trained historians work—using reliable documents from which to reconstruct it. I want to invite everyone into the writing of history, not just academically trained PhDs.

The task before us will be to look at the way various commentators have viewed Powell and his ideas; in doing so, perhaps we will see more truthfully how our own culture in this century has evolved in its ideas about water and land and how those resources should be used. It is important to understand these cultural blinders so that we might recognize and tell our version of the story. If we can read the full arc of the story and understand what shapes its evolution, then we can invent more responsibly the way we think the story—in this case, the story of John Wesley Powell and reclamation in the Colorado River Basin—should be told in the future. More importantly, understanding our storytelling predecessors will help us acknowledge that we, too, are inventing the past for ourselves and our times, not setting it in stone.

To answer the question of what Powell would have thought about these "cash-register dams," we must first begin where all historians begin, with primary sources; that is, with Powell's writings and speeches and other contemporaneous actions relating to the subject. His ideas, as we saw earlier, appear most readily in two publications. As we noted, Powell first laid out his plan for irrigation in the West in 1878 in *Arid Lands Report*; later, in 1890, he elaborated on those ideas in a series of articles in *Century Magazine*.[3] Here are his main points:

1. Powell believed that water scarcity would allow for only 3 percent of the arid West ever to be irrigated.

2. Powell foresaw the day and recommended that essentially every stream and river in the West be developed for irrigation.[4] In no place does he discuss leaving rivers running wild.

3. The development of water resources in the West should involve a cooperative effort of the federal government and local capital. This meant that the government would locate the potential dam sites, as Powell's USGS men began to do in 1889. After this, local cooperative associations, in what he called hydrographic basins, would band together to provide the capital, labor, and rules for establishing and distributing water. (A hydrographic basin is a land unit dependent upon a single or related water source; for example, in the Cedar City area, Cedar Mountain, the eastern Bumblebee Mountains, and Cedar Valley, then, might constitute a hydrographic basin.) Powell modeled his ideas on the Mormon experiment in Utah and other experiments in Colorado, New Mexico, and California. But he specifically and emphatically called for the federal government to stay out of the construction and operation of dams. He says:

[I]n the name of the men who labor I demand that the laborers shall employ themselves; that the enterprise shall be controlled by the men who have the genius to organize and whose homes are in the lands developed, and that the money shall be furnished by the people; and I say to the Government: Hands off! Furnish the people with the institutions of justice, and let them do the work for themselves.[5]

4. His goal in all of this was to provide a means for the small farmer to survive and farm in the West.

5. Finally, he emphatically opposed land and water speculation.

In addition to these "facts," one must also put Powell's words in context, the cultural and personal worlds in which he wrote. As a farmer and a Methodist preacher's son growing up in pre-Civil War America, Powell inherited a belief in the notion of the Jeffersonian yeoman. Our third president had envisioned a nation of farmers supplying goods to European manufacturers; maintaining such an agrarian economy, Jefferson believed, would ensure a morally upright and virtuous nation.[6] Idealist John Wesley Powell concurred. As Powell biographer Wallace Stegner has said, "Somewhere in Major Powell's small, maimed whiskery person there burned some of the Utopian zeal of Brook Farm and New Harmony."[7]

Moreover, the Major believed in Manifest Destiny (the idea that it was Americans' God-given destiny to occupy, conquer, civilize, Anglicize, and Christianize the whole continent). He also believed in what would later become known as geographical determinism (the idea that settlers adapt their culture and institutions to the environment).

And finally, in all of his work on reclamation he had a strong utilitarian impulse. In one of the *Century* articles Powell states, "Conquered rivers are better servants than wild clouds.... all [of the four great western rivers] are to be utilized in the near future for the hosts of men who are repairing to these survey lands."[8]

Before moving to Powell's interpreters, one might need some background on the development of western reclamation in general and Upper Colorado Basin reclamation in particular (the "Upper Colorado Basin" refers to everything above Lees Ferry, Arizona).

When Major Powell died on 23 September 1902, the Reclamation (or Newlands) Act had been law for three months. This act ended a decade of intense debate and lobbying on the part of various western irrigation interests. The strongest of these advocates were William E. Smythe and the International Irrigation Congress. Writing and editing *The Irrigation Age*, Smythe and his associates originally argued for a cession of public lands to the states to help launch irrigation projects funded by private enterprise.

Nevertheless, the movement toward federal reclamation gained momentum with an 1897 report by Captain Hiram Chittenden of the Army Corps of Engineers. After investigating reservoir sites in Wyoming and Colorado, Chittenden recommended federally built and federally owned water works. Not all irrigation advocates immediately jumped on Chittenden's boat, but the waters were flowing that way as the century ended. In 1901 Smythe's successor, George Maxwell, was joined by Frederick Newell of the USGS and Senator Francis Newlands of Nevada to push the issue in front of Congress.[9]

When congressional debate began, many midwestern and eastern congressmen opposed the idea of federal reclamation for a number of reasons: they felt it unfair to aid western farmers at the expense of their eastern counterparts; they believed that future generations would suffer the burden of paying debts for such water projects; they thought that opening these irrigated lands constituted a government subsidy for a few; and they felt that the proposal violated states' rights.

Out west, reclamation advocates countered that the Newlands Act would help extend the frontier and relieve pressure of overcrowding in the cities (this has become known as the "safety valve theory"); that the act would demonstrate wise conservation of a precious resource; that irrigated crops would be consumed locally and not compete with eastern products; that the program would eventually pay for itself; that the legislation would create new markets for eastern manufactured goods (note that Jefferson's agrarian paradise had moved west); and that federal dams in the West were no more paternalistic than Corps of Engineers river and harbor projects in the East.[10] Ultimately under a new, conservation-minded president, Theodore Roosevelt, the act passed, and the federal government entered the dam-building business.[11]

On the Colorado River specifically, the government began its activities even before 1922—the date Colorado Basin states signed the Colorado River Compact. Survey teams led by E. C. LaRue had located the potential dam sites in Cataract Canyon, in Glen Canyon, and on the San Juan River in 1914, 1915, and 1921.[12]

In 1923 LaRue, Claude Birdseye, and Raymond Moore followed in Powell's footsteps, leading a USGS crew through the Grand Canyon noting possible dam sites there.[13] The prime fruit of all this activity arrived when Congress authorized Boulder Dam near Las Vegas. Work commenced in 1930, and the first power from what was then the largest electric power plant in the world began surging in the fall of 1936.[14]

By the Franklin D. Roosevelt era, dam-building in the West was moving along at a feverish pace; it was part of the New Deal's massive conservation program. But more interestingly, the bureau's power within the Interior Department was becoming gargantuan, outsized. Its march to empire status—and by the end of World War II the bureau had clearly become an empire—began when it started to sell hydroelectric power to finance its other irrigation projects.

Needless to say, after the war the pressure increased to build even more dams in the Colorado Basin. The first proposal was for a dam in Dinosaur National Monument near the confluence of the Green and Yampa rivers—a place where both of Powell's river parties had stopped to rest. But a massive publicity and lobbying campaign by Bernard DeVoto, David Brower, and the Sierra Club eventually defeated that proposal in 1955.[15] Many consider this battle the beginnings of modern-day environmental activism.

Nevertheless, the next year the Colorado River Storage Compact was enacted. It projected dams at Flaming Gorge, on the San Juan, in Glen Canyon, and at numerous other places in the Upper Colorado Basin.[16] Those at Flaming Gorge, in Glen Canyon, on the San Juan, and elsewhere went up, of course, but those later proposed for the Grand Canyon at Marble Canyon and Bridge Canyon were defeated in the late 1960s by national popular consensus provoked by Sierra Club action.[17]

From the 1960s to the present many other dams stopped the flows of western rivers, but in 1987 the bureau apparently changed course, announcing that "[i]nstead of constructing big water and power projects, [we will] concentrate on conserving water and assuring good water quality and environmental protection."[18] The era of dam-building in the West seems to have ended, but the debate about these dams and about John Wesley Powell's role in all this rages on.

One of Powell's first interpreters, William E. Smythe in *The Conquest of Arid America* (1899), wrote about him even before the Major's death. Smythe, you will recall, edited *The Irrigation Age* and fought zealously for federal involvement in western irrigation. Placing Powell's name on the roll of irrigation champions, he noted that Powell's Irrigation Survey paved the way for civilizing the desert wilderness.[19] Smythe's faith resembled Powell's in that he felt irrigation could help unify and rejuvenate America. He also saw irrigation as the key to developing the West in accordance with what we have called the safety valve theory—as an antidote to the ills of modern, urban life. Smythe was both a Populist and a Progressive. As a Populist he was arguing for the rights of small farmers who had been crunched by an unscrupulous, post-Civil War economic system; as a Progressive he was participating in a reform movement that reached its apotheosis with Theodore Roosevelt and his Forest Service chief, Gifford Pinchot. Progressive conservation was "the gospel," as Samuel Hays put it, of using natural resources efficiently and wisely so as not to waste them. Rather than rape and plunder, it advocated sustained yield.

Another early Powell interpreter was Powell's crewmate, Frederick S. Dellenbaugh, from the second expedition down the Colorado in 1871–1872. In his *The Romance of the Colorado River* (1902) and especially *A Canyon Voyage* (1908), Dellenbaugh commented extensively on Powell's goals for western reclamation. In the latter book he rejoiced that dam sites all over the West were being identified and that one day even Sockdolager Rapid in the Grand Canyon might be covered over—the first suggestion I know of to dam the Grand Canyon.[20] Dellenbaugh saw himself and Powell as a first wave of exploration, as the conquering frontiersmen, after whom the frontier inevitably would be tamed. They saw it wild and suffered its hardships even while imbibing its wonders—all so that other men could more easily settle and civilize the lands. A passage from his introduction to *A Canyon Voyage* suggests his basic attitudes:

In the dark night beside some roaring fall, with the thun-
der crashing as if those towering walls were tumbling from
their heights; with the lightening flashing ... and the rain
descending in torrential floods that leap and gather from
the confining precipices, one truly feels in the very heart
of elemental nature, and ... marvels that man has survived
the constant onslaught of storm and fire, and is ... able not
merely to protect himself, but even to utilize the annihilat-
ing forces for ... his own comfort.[21]

The world Dellenbaugh describes here is a Spencerian world of
struggle, of the survival of the fittest. That late-nineteenth-century
social theory derived from Darwin's biological theories and came
to be called Social Darwinism. Herbert Spencer envisioned life as a
struggle against a hostile universe, and his theories ultimately influenced two or three generations of Euro-American scientists, writers, philosophers, psychologists, and others. For Dellenbaugh and
his contemporaries, conquering the West would manifest the destiny
of the most "fit" race on the earth—white Americans. His imperial-
ist, if not racist, views on conquest suggest very much the spirit of
the western movement during the whole nineteenth century.

A decade or so after Dellenbaugh, George Wharton James in
Reclaiming the Arid West (1917) provided one of the most interesting
and original, if confused, portraits of Powell and his work on reclamation. James was a defrocked minister-turned-desert-promoter
and writer. As befit his ministerial background, James spoke of Powell as a prophet and called him everything *but* Moses. James's language is so full of hyperbole and zeal that one must listen to it to
appreciate it. He says of the Major:

He visualized before me so that I also saw them, these dams
being erected, those canals excavated ... and his face shone
with a light of transfiguration.... he was essentially a democratic leader, nay, more, a bishop, a shepherd, a guide to
the great ... flock of men, women and children who were
never to know him personally, but who were to feel ... the
all-urging love of his great heart.[22]

James reinvented Powell as the prophet who never saw the promised land—a theme on which Walter Prescott Webb and Wallace Stegner later expanded.

Most significantly for our subject, James claimed that Powell grasped the vastness of the reclamation enterprise and saw that *only* the federal government could undertake such a project.[23] Dellenbaugh, Smythe, and others had suggested as much, but none had said it as baldly as James.[24] Living in an era of rapid expansion, industrialization, and optimism, James wanted others to see Powell as the hero who had led them there.

Despite Smythe, Dellenbaugh, James, and others, by the end of the 1920s Powell was largely a forgotten figure. In the Modernist era of H.L. Mencken, Ezra Pound, and T.S. Eliot, a government bureaucrat like Powell who was concerned with the rural West did not fire the imaginations of these movers and shakers of 1920s American culture. To them the city and its accompanying sense of irony and sophistication were what mattered. Modernists were generally moral relativists who often expressed a skeptical, world-weary outlook on life. Moreover, they looked to the city, because of its complexity and excitement, as the repository of the real world's values, such as they were. It was in and against such a cultural milieu that Walter Prescott Webb wrote *The Great Plains* (1931), as much an antidote to Modernism as it has become a classic in environmental history.

In this book Webb theorized that when forest-dwelling America stumbled onto the plains it bumped up against an alien landscape—semiarid, treeless, and flat. Yet ultimately these Americans found new ways to survive there. Those who stayed did so by adapting themselves to the environment, and there followed what Powell had called a "new phase of Aryan civilization."[25] Webb so admired Powell's earlier ideas about adapting one's farming methods and institutions to the arid lands environment, that he began his book with this very quote about Aryan civilization.

Webb devoted considerable space to Powell and his reclamation programs. And he noted, in opposition to what James and earlier commentators had said, that Powell did not advocate federal involvement in dam construction. But Webb went on to add that Powell's idea was problematic because irrigation is "by its nature an interstate matter."[26] In other words, Webb implied that Powell *should* have favored federalism. On the whole, however, Webb endorsed Powell and his ideas, especially because Powell championed the interests of Webb's beloved western farmer. Webb scholar Gregory Tobin says that Webb wrote *The Great Plains* in large part to explain and glorify the agricultural and pastoral world in west Texas from which he had come. It was a retort, Tobin says, to the then-current trend to venerate the urban East.[27]

Although Webb does not say so directly in *The Great Plains*, he described Powell as a nascent New Dealer who had tried to reverse the trend of government favoring eastern business interests against the South and West. Webb himself later supported New Deal policies and wrote one of his most famous books, *Divided We Stand*, to rebuff the Northeast and back what Webb saw as the New Deal's concern for the common man. Nonetheless, in rediscovering the significance of his western rural roots, one might say that for a whole generation of historians and lay readers, Walter Prescott Webb rediscovered John Wesley Powell.

Immediately after World War II and at the end of the New Deal era came a number of important studies that championed Powell. In *The Literary Fallacy* (1944), Bernard DeVoto took up Webb's ideas about Powell and related them to modern literature.[28] Henry Nash Smith's seminal work on the West as symbol and myth, *The Virgin Land* (1950), offered Powell as the hero for a new type of western myth in place of the old cowboy myth and the Frederick Jackson Turner frontier thesis.[29] Both DeVoto and Smith in turn influenced the first two extended studies of Powell to appear: William Culp Darrah's biography, *Powell of the Colorado* (1951), and Wallace Stegner's study of Powell's public career, *Beyond the Hundredth Meridian: John Wesley Powell and the Second Opening of the West* (1954).

Darrah wrote as a Franklin D. Roosevelt conservationist and thus as a believer in the federal government's work in the West. He claimed that Powell envisioned great storage dams on the Colorado. He said that Boulder Dam rests near a site Powell had long ago considered feasible.[30] Darrah also stated that for twenty-five years Powell had argued for a Federal Bureau of Irrigation similar to the agency created in 1902, the Bureau of Reclamation.[31] In many ways he fell into line with other Powell interpreters. Because he believed so strongly that the Bureau of Reclamation was helping the small farmer that Powell wanted to help, Darrah was willing to stretch the story's skin to cover his own beliefs. In reality Powell had never talked about a dam near Boulder Canyon, and Darrah had nothing to document his statement. But like his predecessors, he imagined an "evolved" Powell; that is, Darrah and others believed that Powell, had he been living in the 1940s and 1950s, would undoubtedly have approved of these kinds of bureau projects. So Darrah made him more usable to the present.

For a different purpose, Wallace Stegner followed a similar track of inventing an updated Powell. But what Stegner did that is germane to our study was to lead Powell out of the Bureau of Reclamation corral into which previous commentators had driven him. While Stegner joined his predecessors in calling Powell an unheeded prophet, he distinguished between Powell's reclamation program and the bureau's. Powell's work may have resulted in the bureau, but that was not the Major's intent. According to Stegner, the juggernaut just happened to evolve that way.

He went on to say that Powell would have very much opposed the way that the bureau had become an empire unto itself. In the conclusion to *Beyond the Hundredth Meridian*, Stegner strongly asserted that Powell "might join the Sierra Club and other conservation groups in deploring some proposed and 'feasible' dams such as that in Echo Park... and he might agree that considerations such as recreation, wildlife protection, preservation for the future of untouched wilderness, might sometimes outweigh possible irrigation and power benefits."[32] If Powell ever said this in a publication, a letter, a journal, or a speech, I have never read it.[33] Still, Stegner's use of the term "might" suggests he was imagining Powell living and working in the post-World War II era. At least Stegner partially recognized his own bias here. Nonetheless, Stegner's interpretation profoundly affected the way Powell was viewed. Stegner had grown a new tree called Powell whose leaves now looked suspiciously preservationist.

To understand why he did this, one must bear in mind Stegner's times and the issues he was personally involved in as a Sierra Club member. Along with David Brower and the Sierra Club, Stegner opposed the Echo Park Dam. Brower eventually persuaded Stegner to edit and write part of the book *This Is Dinosaur*. It was the first in a series of Sierra Club books used as a propaganda tool, in this case for the club's campaign to thwart the Bureau of Reclamation at Echo Park in Dinosaur National Monument.

Perhaps more importantly, remember that Stegner was writing at the beginning of the Eisenhower administration, which was attempting to give away federal lands to states for redistribution to private individuals. Stegner likened this to the land-grab maneuverings of Powell's nemesis, Nevada senator William Stewart. In fact, in Stegner's story one could easily substitute someone like Eisenhower's Interior secretary Douglas McKay (an Oregon Chevrolet dealer known in environmental circles as "Giveaway McKay") in Stewart's place, and his book would read more or less the same. Stegner writes, "The forces that he [Powell] fought all during his public life are, as of 1953, not only still there but active and aggressive.... A public land policy that a few years before [during Franklin D. Roosevelt's administration] had looked reasonably consistent and settled was in danger of complete overturn."[34]

In Powell's time Mammon and Greed had threatened the republic; in Stegner's time they threatened again. Stegner was asking his readers to heed the prophet this time and thwart the William Stewarts of his own era. While Stegner no doubt knew that Powell probably never wrote a preservationist word in his life, Stegner imagined that Powell, had he lived in the 1950s, would have evolved into a preservationist of sorts.

With Stegner's book the road on Powell had split, just as the conservation movement itself had done. Up until the postwar period, conservation had been closely allied with western water development and that meant the Bureau of Reclamation. In his groundbreaking book, *Conservation and the Gospel of Efficiency*, Samuel Hays states that the term "conversation" and the movement itself actually derived from the Reclamation Act.[35] Now, however, conservation was joining a new set of friends. Connate with this, the discussion of Powell, like environmental issues in general, was wandering out of the drawing rooms of high culture and into the living rooms of popular culture.

Stegner's book earned considerable attention and helped popularize Powell and the issues of dams versus wild rivers. But more to the point, *Beyond the Hundredth Meridian* established Powell as a guide figure for a second side in a very fierce and ongoing battle about water in the West. Powell had once stood for a Bureau of Reclamation that had aligned itself with the little man against corruption, big business, and the like. Now he was standing against that same bureau. But this bureau, according to Stegner and others, had become the pawn of the very enemies it had sought to foil.

Stegner notwithstanding, the bureau and reclamationists held to their version of the Colorado River's first explorer as a "Bureau Man." As we noted at the beginning of this section, the Bureau of Reclamation named its largest reservoir after him (as suggested by Platt Cline, editor of Flagstaff's *Arizona Daily Sun.*)[36] And the bureau's films and publications on Glen Canyon continue to view Powell as an approving father figure. Among other references to and icons of Powell at Glen Canyon, his bronze image sits on the transformer deck looking up at the massive concrete structure.[37]

Meanwhile, the Sierra Club, the leading environmental group of the period, had other notions about Powell. Their popular publications depicted a very different image of him, particularly for the generation that came of age in the 1960s. Moreover, Stegner's book on Powell became a sort of Sierra Club standard and, later, as the club opposed dams in Glen and Grand canyons, Stegner's comments on Powell were frequently quoted.

Author Francois Leydet cited them in the Sierra Club's Grand Canyon book, *Time and the River Flowing.*[38] Likewise, in the Club's publication on Glen Canyon, *The Place No One Knew*, editor Brower and author Eliot Porter used lines from Powell's *Exploration of the Colorado of the West* to complement images designed to mourn what Glen Canyon Dam was destroying. Brower intoned that "Eliot Porter's name will be inseparable from the spirit of Glen Canyon, just as John Wesley Powell's is from the discovery of the Canyon."[39] The message was clear: Powell would have joined the club in opposing this dam.

Out of the Sierra Club tradition arose an author who has spurred environmental activism in the Southwest more than anyone before or since. I am talking about Edward Abbey, the author of *Desert Solitaire, The Journey Home, The Monkey Wrench Gang, The Hidden Canyon*, and other popular works about the Colorado Plateau. Abbey claimed Powell as one of the good guys in the environmental fight. In his essay "Down the River with Major Powell," he associates Powell with the pre-dam pristine beauty of Glen Canyon and implies that the Colorado's first explorer would have opposed any such alterations of the place.[40] In *The Hidden Canyon*, a journal account of a river trip Abbey took through the Grand Canyon, he juxtaposes his own journal entries with quotes from Powell's *Exploration*. At the end of that book Abbey says that "Glen Canyon was part of our river before and shall be again.... Glen Canyon Dam must fall.... the spirit of John Wesley Powell will understand.... Listen to his words."[41]

Taking his cue from the Sierra Club and Stegner (Abbey was Stegner's student in Stanford's creative writing program), Abbey invented Powell as a 1960s environmentalist. Furthermore, coinciding with the publication of Abbey's books was the centennial celebration of Powell's first trip down the Colorado in 1869. People were buying Powell's *Exploration of the Colorado River of the West* by the thousands. A beautifully written book, *Exploration* impressed many readers with the idea that Powell loved wild rivers. Southwest river runners consider it a bible of sorts and look upon Powell as the god-figure who wrote it.

In popular culture these extreme views of Powell still exist, but not quite so among academic historians. One outgrowth of Stegner, Brower, Sierra Club activism, and the burgeoning environmental movement of the 1960s and 1970s was an emerging academic field now known as environmental history.[42] Three historians from the field have discussed Powell's role in western irrigation and the confusion arising therefrom: Donald Worster in *Rivers of Empire* (1985); Marc Reisner in *Cadillac Desert* (1986); and Patricia Nelson Limerick in *Desert Passages* (1985).

Of the three, Limerick takes most notice of the debate about Powell. She asserts that how one feels about Powell's stand on reclamation depends on which of Powell's two famous works now in print one reads—*Exploration* or the *Arid Lands Report*. Calling Powell a "less-than-manageable founding father" for both preservationists and reclamationists, she states that Powell's "landscape of appreciation and his landscape of use were simply different places."[43] At first glance this seems a satisfactory explanation, yet even this interpretation ignores certain aspects of Powell's times. Actually, Powell's aesthetic landscape conflated with his utilitarian landscape. Aesthetic appreciation of a river was a spiritual *use* for Powell just as reclamation was a material *use*. Both uses formed part of his basically human-centered view toward land.

Just when Limerick thought she had resolved the debate, her penchant for polar arguments and her limited research ignored an important feature of Powell's personality and outlook. It appears as if that leaves us floating down the river without a life jacket. Fortunately, Worster is more prescient about Powell when he points out what a complex and polymath person Powell was. Worster defines four different and seemingly contradictory Powells that writers have invented in their study of him.[44] I will come back to these shortly.

If we return to the original question I posed at the beginning, we ask if Powell would have approved of these cash-register dams and especially, if he would have approved of Glen Canyon Dam? The Powell I invent to answer this question will come from both history and myth, from primary sources and my own values.

First, let us recognize that Powell never said anywhere that he would oppose dams on the Colorado River. As we saw, he would have dammed any water source in the West if it brought water to the small farmer. But for numerous reasons he did not envision dams in deep canyons. One reason is that the technology of his time would have allowed neither the construction of dams in such places nor the pumping of water up and over the canyon walls to waiting farmers.[45] Another is that he could not imagine a cooperative association funding and constructing such massive undertakings. But no canyon was sacred to him, nor was any river or wilderness; at least no records exist stating such. So in that sense, I would answer a very qualified yes to our question.

Second, considering that he wanted small dams controlled by local groups for the good of those people only, and also considering that he wanted to keep the federal government out of reclamation and avoid "empire building," Powell would have especially lamented the empire the Bureau of Reclamation became. Here Stegner comes closer to the truth, I think, in the sense that Powell would have opposed Glen Canyon and other Colorado Basin dams with all his considerable powers of persuasion and scientific acumen.

But these answers are not quite complete, because for me no clear image of Powell has emerged in our time *for* our time. So we still have to invent the kind of Powell we want for the future, based on the information we now have before us, knowing what has happened in the past. Since we cannot have the Major walk from off-stage, as Woody Allen had Marshall McLuhan do in Allen's movie *Annie Hall*, we will have to rely on the sources before us and our own sense of what the times demand.

I have a version of Powell that I would like to invent. Granting that history and myth do converge, I would submit that perhaps my John Wesley Powell is the one we might want to talk about for the next few decades. In other words, I have a story of John Wesley Powell and it goes like this (here I am borrowing from Donald Worster's four Powells): the last Powell that Worster defines is the midwestern-born farmer who wanted arid lands agriculture built on similar foundations to his own—with decentralized, democratic institutions where ordinary people controlled their own lives. As Worster points out, this is the least-known Powell and the one most needed today.[46] I agree.

As for the way I will go about finding my Powell, I see little wrong with the methodology that historians use to study the past. While all ways of knowing have their limits, this method of searching primary and secondary sources is a most responsible way of trying to learn about the past. But more important than my methodology, let me stress my essential bias right here. I consider myself a responsible historian, but know that I *am* an environmentalist.

In inventing my Powell I first recognize that Powell's notion of hydrographic basins was a very important first step toward the understanding of what are now called bioregions. A bioregion constitutes a part of the earth with similar patterns of plant and animal life, and similar climatic and geographical characteristics. The Colorado Plateau, or what Powell called "The Plateau Province," might be called a bioregion. Bioregionalists urge us to inhabit these regions with a sensitivity to the life patterns found there, and to make economic decisions that maintain the integrity of the region's life systems.[47] So let's call Powell, not a bioregionalist, but a precursor to that notion.[48]

Then let us recognize that Powell opposed empire building—in the private and public sectors—and that what happened with the Bureau of Reclamation after his death was not his plan at all. He believed in decentralized, self-determined groups of people working out and controlling their own futures. He also believed in the small farmer and the small anything; for the Major, big was not better. As he said in "Institutions for the Arid Lands": "The building of great industrial operations does not daze my vision. I love the cradle more than the bank counter. The cottage home is more beautiful to me than the palace."[49] Like Jefferson and like most environmentalists, Powell abhorred the notion of America becoming a big industrial power.

Let us take those notions of smallness and bioregionalism, again recognizing the difference between the words that came out of Powell's mouth and the words we have put into it. Let us wed bioregionalism and smallness to the sense of awe and wonder that he clearly felt when he looked out over the Colorado Plateau. And let us recognize that while aesthetic appreciation in itself does not an environmentalist make, it can be a beginning. Let us imagine, then, as I think Stegner has done, that Powell just might have worn environmentalist clothing had he grown up in the post-World War II era rather than the pre-Civil War period. And let us take Powell's sense of awe further than he did and say that it could lead to an understanding that humans are not the center of the universe (Powell saw the world anthropocentrically) and that we need to exercise more caution in how we think about and act toward land and water in the West and everywhere else. Powell, after all, *was* a very humble, cautious man; his Irrigation Survey epitomized restraint and caution. So he might have developed an understanding of the humility and restraint that environmentalism espouses. And if he saw that the common good now means something else, something expanded from what it meant in the 1880s, then as one of the most curious and intelligent minds of his time, he would probably be intrigued with the idea were he living in our time.

With both hands held before you I give you my John Wesley Powell. In these hands I hope you see some of what he was, how others have seen him, and why I see him as I do. And if I could see what may hover behind my back in the form of an invisible agenda, I would give you that as well. But of course, that is exactly the task before all of us, the task of all historians and all students of history.

A fixed version of Powell and the past does not serve us very well. We require a Powell and a past with which we can continually interact, as well as a recognition that we do interact with him.[50] Indeed, I believe our nineteenth-century hero is alive and well in the twenty-first century. Somewhere down the river ahead of us, red-haired, one-armed John Wesley Powell waits, beckoning us to follow.

4   Conclusion

The Powell surveys between 1869 and 1875 added considerably to American science and to America's sense of itself and its land. Powell developed some important theories of mountain building and erosion (which his fellow survey members, Grove Karl Gilbert and Clarence E. Dutton, developed further and published). He also basically invented the field of physiography, or physical geology. His (and Almon H. Thompson's) maps not only filled in the last blank spot on the U.S. map, they also set a new standard for cartography and helped pave the way in 1879 for the United States Geological Survey, whose main task was mapping.

Powell also developed revolutionary ideas about arid-lands settlement, based on his astute observations about where and how rivers like the Green, the Colorado, the San Juan, and their tributaries could be irrigated. His "pioneering ethnographic research" on the Nuche—the Numic-speaking Shoshoneans of the Intermountain West—was groundbreaking and "remarkably devoid of Eurocentric biases," according to archaeologist Jerry Spangler.[1] That work formed a baseline of ethnographic information about the Nuche. Such research helped shape the Bureau of American Ethnology. Powell conceived of the bureau and served as its first director, also in 1879.

Likewise, much of the work of Powell's crews on the expeditions proved groundbreaking as well. Thompson went on to become chief cartographer for the USGS. E. O. Beaman's photographs of the Green and Colorado were the first images of these canyons and established baseline photographs for subsequent geologists, hydrologists, photographers, and botanists doing comparative Colorado Basin studies along the rivers; a few ended up in eastern parlors as stereopticon images. Jack Hillers became chief photographer for the USGS and is acknowledged as one of the greats in western photography. Powell set a high standard for scientific studies of the water in the West; these studies continue today. He also raised many of the issues about dams and water development in the West that the twentieth century's Bureau of Reclamation would both take up and ignore.

The West that Powell had sought to settle in a rational, scientific manner based on the conditions of the environment had, in the Turnerian terms which Powell endorsed, officially closed shortly before his death. His vision, however, did not fully guide that settlement. Much suffering and failure attended whites' settling of the West, in good part because of the myths that Powell had fought against. Nevertheless, Powell bequeathed to the nation a legacy of fearless exploration, brilliant science, and dedicated public service. His gravestone at Arlington National Cemetery sums up his career well: "Soldier. Explorer. Scientist." One might also add "Writer." With his account of his 1869 voyage down the Colorado, he left us one of the great adventure stories in American literature.

Notes

NOTES TO CHAPTER 1, BIOGRAPHY

1. Mrs. M. D. Lincoln, "John Wesley Powell," *Open Court* 16, 17 (December 1902–February 1903): 706.
2. Lincoln, 706–8; William Culp Darrah, *Powell of the Colorado* (1951; repr., Princeton: Princeton University Press, 1970), 6–16.
3. Lindsey Gardner Morris, "John Wesley Powell: Scientist and Educator," *Illinois State University Journal* 31.3 (February 1969): 16.
4. Darrah, *Powell*, 81–82.
5. Wallace Stegner, "Jack Sumner and John Wesley Powell," *Colorado Magazine* 26 (1949): 61–69.
6. John Wesley Powell, "Press Release," 1890 Water Resource Division Records of Powell Survey Concerning Field Operations, 1889–1890, RG 57, Document #121, National Archives, Washington, DC, p. 3.
7. Donald Worster, *A River Running West: The Life of John Wesley Powell* (New York: Oxford University Press, 2001), 157.
8. See Eilean Adams, *Hell or High Water: James White's Disputed Passage through the Grand Canyon, 1867* (Logan: Utah State University Press, 2001), for a recent accounting of all the evidence about White's claim. See also Harold A. Bulger, "First Man through the Grand Canyon," *Missouri Historical Society Bulletin* 17.4 (July 1961): 321–31.
9. W. H. Brewer, "John Wesley Powell," *American Journal of Science* 14

(1902): 381.

10. John Wesley Powell, *The Exploration of the Colorado River and Its Canyons*, originally published in 1895 as *Canyons of the Colorado* (New York: Dover, 1961), 8.

11. Robert Brewster Stanton, *Colorado River Controversies* (1932; repr., Boulder City, NV: Westwater Books, 1982), 147, 177.

12. Michael P. Ghiglieri, *First through Grand Canyon: The Secret Journals and Letters of the 1869 Crew Who Explored the Green and Colorado Rivers* (Flagstaff, AZ: Puma Press, 2003), 111.

13. Ibid., 188.

14. Ibid., 197.

15. Powell, *Exploration*, 75–76.

16. Ghiglieri, *First*, 204.

17. Ibid., 215.

18. Ibid., 222.

19. Ibid., 224.

20. See Jay Haymond and John F. Hoffman, "Interview with Otis 'Dock' Marston," May 1976, Utah State Historical Society, Salt Lake City; and Wesley P. Larsen, "The Letter, or Were Powell's People Really Killed by Indians," *Canyon Legacy* 17 (Spring 1993): 12–18.

21. Mary C. Rabbitt et al., *The Colorado Region and John Wesley Powell*, U.S. Geological Survey Professional Paper 669 (Washington, DC: GPO, 1969), 7.

22. William Morris Davis, "Biographical Memoir of John Wesley Powell, 1834–1902," *National Academy of Sciences* 8 (February 1915): 29.

23. Darrah, *Powell*, 152–53.

24. Frederick Dellenbaugh, *A Canyon Voyage: A Narrative of the Second Powell Expedition Down the Green–Colorado River from Wyoming, and the Exploration on Land, in the Years 1871 and 1872* (1908; repr., New Haven: Yale University Press, 1962), 243.

25. Wallace Stegner, *Beyond the Hundredth Meridian: John Wesley Powell and the Second Opening of the West* (1954; repr., Lincoln: University of Nebraska Press, 1982), 146.

26. Ibid., 189.

27. For a complete study of Holmes's life and work, see Kevin J. Fernlund, *William Henry Holmes and the Rediscovery of the American West* (Albuquerque: University of New Mexico Press, 2000).

28. Stegner, *Beyond*, 254.

29. Darrah, *Powell*, 221.

30. For a study of all four federal surveys, see Richard A. Bartlett, *The Great Surveys of the West* (Norman: University of Oklahoma Press, 1962). For a thorough biography of F. V. Hayden, see Mike Foster, *Strange Genius: The Life of Ferdinand Vandeveer Hayden* (Niwot, CO: Roberts Rinehart Publishers, 1994).

31. Henry Nash Smith, "Clarence King, John Wesley Powell, and the Establishment of the United States Geological Survey," *Mississippi Valley Historical Review* 34 (1947): 52.
32. Davis, "Biographical Memoir," 55.
33. Darrah, *Powell*, 301.
34. Ibid., 310.
35. For a summary of all Powell's ideas about irrigation and western lands see John Wesley Powell, "Institutions for the Arid Lands," *Century* 40 (1890): 111–16; Powell, "The Irrigable Lands of the Arid Region," *Century* 39 (1890): 766–76; Powell, "The Non-Irrigable Lands of the Arid Region," *Century* 39 (1890): 915–22.
36. Thomas G. Alexander, *A Clash of Interests: Interior Department and Mountain West, 1863–96* (Provo: Brigham Young University Press, 1977), 155.
37. Darrah, *Powell*, 350–51.
38. Worster, *A River Running West*, 544.
39. Ibid., 354.

NOTES TO CHAPTER 2, INTERPRETING POWELL'S WRITINGS ON EXPLORATION, LAND PLANNING, AND ANTHROPOLOGY

1. Grove Karl Gilbert, "John Wesley Powell," *Open Court* 17 (1903): 289.
2. Ibid., 287.
3. Ibid., 289.
4. Powell, *Exploration*, x.
5. William H. Goetzmann and William N. Goetzmann, *The West of the Imagination* (New York: W. W. Norton, 1986), 12.
6. Powell, *Exploration*, 394.
7. Ibid., 7.
8. Ibid.
9. John G. Cawelti, *Adventure, Mystery and Romance: Formula Stories as Art and Popular Culture* (Chicago: University of Chicago Press, 1976), 40.
10. Joseph Campbell, *The Hero with a Thousand Faces*, 2nd ed. (Princeton: Princeton University Press, 1968), 30.
11. Cawelti, *Adventure*, 40.
12. Powell, *Exploration*, 99.
13. Campbell, *The Hero*, 92.
14. Powell, *Exploration*, 80.
15. Ibid., 104.
16. Ibid., 129.
17. Ibid., 126.
18. Campbell, *The Hero*, 40.
19. Powell, *Exploration*, 89.

20. Otis "Dock" Marston, ed., "The Lost Journal of John Colton Sumner," *Utah Historical Quarterly* 37 (Spring 1969): 177.

21. William Culp Darrah, ed., "Exploration of the Colorado River in 1869," *Utah Historical Quarterly* 15 (1947): 21.

22. For a discussion of the use of the palimpsest metaphor in discussing nature, see Michael P. Cohen, *The Pathless Way: John Muir and American Wilderness* (Madison: University of Wisconsin Press, 1984), 104–9.

23. Stegner, *Beyond*, 170–71.

24. Paul Shepard, *Man in the Landscape: A Historic View of the Esthetics of Nature* (New York: Alfred A. Knopf, 1967), 245.

25. Ibid.

26. Powell, *Exploration*, 76.

27. Worster, *A River Running West*, 334.

28. John Wesley Powell, *Report on the Lands of the Arid Region of the United States with a More Detailed Account of the Lands of Utah*, ed. T. H. Watkins (1878; repr., Boston: Harvard Common Press, 1983), 29.

29. Alexander, *A Clash of Interests*, 155.

30. Stegner, *Beyond*, 258. See also Neil M. Judd, *The Bureau of American Ethnology: A Partial History* (Norman: University of Oklahoma Press, 1967), 3–21.

31. Marvin Harris, *The Rise of Anthropological Theory: A History of Theories of Culture* (New York: Thomas Y. Crowell Co., 1968), 100–1.

32. Ibid., 81.

33. Worster, *A River Running West*, 455.

34. Ibid.

35. Don D. Fowler and Catherine S. Fowler, eds., *The Anthropology of the Numa: John Wesley Powell's Manuscripts of the Numic Peoples of the Western United States, 1868–1880* (Washington, DC: Smithsonian Institution Press, 1971), 19.

NOTES TO CHAPTER 3, INTERPRETATIONS OF POWELL ON IRRIGATION

1. They are often called "cash-register dams" because primarily they produce hydroelectric power to help fund other Bureau of Reclamation projects; they do not provide irrigation water, although they do help control flood waters and silt build-up downstream.

2. Stephen Tatum, *Inventing Billy The Kid: Visions of the Outlaw in America, 1881–1891* (Albuquerque: University of New Mexico Press, 1982), 174.

3. *Report on the Lands of the Arid Region*; "The Irrigable Lands of the Arid Region," *Century* 39 (April 1890): 766–76; "The Non-Irrigable Lands of the Arid Region," *Century* 39 (April 1890): 915–22; and "Institutions for the Arid Lands," *Century* 40 (May 1890): 111–16.

4. Powell, "Press Release," 3.

5. Powell, "Institutions for the Arid Lands," 113.

6. "Notes on Virginia," *Basic Writing of Thomas Jefferson*, ed. Philip S. Foner (New York: Willey Book Co., 1944), 161–62.

7. Stegner, *Beyond*, 316.

8. Powell, "The Irrigable Lands of the Arid Region," 767–68.

9. Michael Robinson, *Water for the West: The Bureau of Reclamation 1902–1977* (Chicago: Public Works Historical Society, 1979), 13–15.

10. Ibid., 15–16.

11. Samuel Hays in *Conservation and the Gospel of Efficiency: The Progressive Conservation Movement 1880–1920* (Cambridge: Harvard University Press, 1959), 5, argues that the term "conservation" itself arose from the movement to construct reservoirs and "conserve" spring floodwaters. Thus from the beginning, conservation meant dam-building—something that might make environmentalists pause when they think to call themselves "conservationists."

12. E. C. LaRue, *The Colorado River and Its Utilization*, U.S. Geological Survey Water Supply Paper 395 (Washington, DC: GPO, 1916), and *Water Power and Flood Control of Colorado River Below Green River, Utah*, U.S. Geological Survey Water Supply Paper 556 (Washington, DC: GPO, 1925).

13. David Lavender, *River Runners of the Grand Canyon* (Grand Canyon, AZ: Grand Canyon Natural History Association, 1985), 59.

14. Marc Reisner, *Cadillac Desert: The American West and Its Disappearing Water* (New York: Viking, 1986), 135–36.

15. See Mark W. T. Harvey, *A Symbol of Wilderness: Echo Park and the American Conservation Movement* (Albuquerque: University of New Mexico Press, 1994), for a thorough study of this controversy. Bernard DeVoto's "Shall We Let Them Ruin Our National Parks?" *Saturday Evening Post* 223 (July 22, 1950): 17–19, 42–48, sparked the debate about Echo Park. Without his prompting, the dam's defeat may never have happened.

16. William E. Warne, *The Bureau of Reclamation* (New York: Praeger, 1973), 248–49.

17. Roderick Nash, *Wilderness and the American Mind*, 3rd ed. (New Haven: Yale University Press, 1982), 230.

18. Philip Shabecoff, "U.S. Bureau for Water Projects Shifts Focus to Conservation," *New York Times*, 2 October 1987, p. 11.

19. William E. Smythe, *The Conquest of Arid America* (1899; repr., Seattle: University of Washington Press, 1969), 261, 263–64.

20. Dellenbaugh, *A Canyon Voyage*, xxxv.

21. Ibid., xxxvi.

22. George Wharton James, *Reclaiming the Arid West: The Story of the United States Reclamation Service* (New York: Dodd, Mead and Company, 1917), xiv–xv.

23. Ibid., 2.

24. See Frederick H. Newell (the first Reclamation Service director), *Irri-*

gation in the United States, 3rd ed. (New York: Thomas Y. Crowell Co., 1906), iv, espousing a similar view of Powell as did James, Dellenbaugh, and Smythe.

25. "The Non-Irrigable Lands of the Arid Region," 922.
26. Walter Prescott Webb, *The Great Plains* (1931; repr., Lincoln: University of Nebraska Press, 1976), 86.
27. Gregory Tobin, *The Making of History: Walter Prescott Webb and "The Great Plains"* (Austin: University of Texas Press, 1976), 86.
28. Bernard DeVoto, *The Literary Fallacy* (1944; repr., Port Washington, NY: Kennikat Press, 1969), 125–35.
29. Henry Nash Smith, *The Virgin Land: The American West as Symbol and Myth* (1950; repr., Cambridge: Harvard University Press, 1978), 196–200.
30. Darrah, *Powell*, 397. Norris Hundley in *Water and the West: The Colorado River Compact and the Politics of Water in the West* (Berkley: University of California Press, 1975), 9, asserts that Powell never said a word about damming the river near the Boulder Canyon area. I have found nothing to contradict Hundley's statement.
31. Darrah, *Powell*, 396.
32. Stegner, *Beyond*, 361.
33. See P. C. Warman, "Catalogue of the Published Writings of John Wesley Powell," *Proceedings of the Washington Academy of Sciences* 5 (July 18, 1903): 131–87, for a nearly complete bibliography of Powell's publications. See also Marcia L. Thomas, *John Wesley Powell: An Annotated Bibliography* (Westport, CT: Praeger, 2004), and Worster, *A River Running West*, 625, 636–38.
34. Stegner, *Beyond*, 357.
35. Hays, *Conservation*, 5.
36. Platt Cline, telephone interview by the author, Cedar City, 20 January 1987. Cline says that his editorial in the *Arizona Daily Sun* in 1957 first suggested applying Powell's name to the reservoir behind the dam that was just then under construction. Thereafter he sent letters to the Interior secretary, to the bureau, and to Arizona and Utah politicians. Apparently the bureau had planned to name the reservoir after a former bureau director, but they took up Cline's suggestion with enthusiasm.
37. See Bureau of Reclamation, *Operation Glen Canyon: The Construction of Glen Canyon Dam*, film, n.d.; Department of the Interior news release, "1969 Centennial Will Honor Major John Wesley Powell," Nov. 19, 1967; Bureau of Reclamation, *Lake Powell: Jewel of the Colorado* (Washington, DC: GPO, 1965); and Stan Jones, *Glen Canyon Dam and Steel Arch Bridge* (Page, AZ: Sun Country Publications, 1984).
38. Francois Leydet, *Time and the River Flowing: Grand Canyon* (San Francisco: Sierra Club Books, 1964), 130.
39. Eliot Porter, *The Place No One Knew: Glen Canyon on the Colorado* (San Francisco: Sierra Club Books, 1963), 7.

40. Edward Abbey, *The Journey Home: Some Words in Defense of the American West* (New York: E. P. Dutton, 1977), 200–2; also see *Desert Solitaire: A Season in the Wilderness* (1968; repr. Layton, UT: Peregrine Smith Books, 1981), 168, 186.

41. Edward Abbey, *The Hidden Canyon: A River Journey* (New York: Viking, 1977), 111.

42. For a history of the field, see Richard White, "American Environmental History: The Development of a New Historical Field," *Pacific Historical Review* 54 (August 1985): 297–335; and Donald Worster, "History as Natural History: An Essay on Theory and Method," *Pacific Historical Review* 53 (February 1984): 1–19.

43. Patricia Nelson Limerick, *Desert Passages: Encounters with the American Deserts* (Albuquerque: University of New Mexico Press, 1985), 172.

44. Donald Worster, *Rivers of Empire: Water, Aridity and the Growth of the American West* (New York: Pantheon Books, 1985), 133. His four Powells are: (1) the wild-river enthusiast; (2) the technocrat who wanted to plan the world; (3) the dedicated bureaucrat whose *Arid Lands Report* was a model of ecological realism; and (4) the midwestern-born farmer who wanted a decentralized, democratic arid lands agriculture where people took charge of their own lives.

45. See Powell, *Report on the Lands of the Arid Region*, 7.

46. Worster is open about his Populist, anticapitalist bias.

47. Peter Berg and Raymond Dasmann, "Reinhabiting California," in *Reinhabiting a Separate Country: A Bioregional Anthology of Northern California*, ed. Peter Berg (San Francisco: Planet Drum Books, 1978), 217–20.

48. Worster, *Rivers of Empire*, 133, also calls attention to this idea.

49. Powell, "Institutions for the Arid Lands," 116.

50. David Lowenthal, *The Past Is a Foreign Country* (Cambridge: Cambridge University Press, 1985), 410.

CHAPTER 4, CONCLUSION

1. Jerry D. Spangler, "The Ute Historic Period: Ethnohistoric and Ethnographic Observations in the Uinta Basin and Tavaputs Plateau, A.D. 1650 to Present," Chapter 12, "Paradigms and Perspectives Revisited: A Class I Overview of the Uinta Basin and Tavaputs Plateau," (report prepared for the Vernal office, Bureau of Land Management, 2002), 19–20.

Selected Bibliography

SELECTED WORKS BY JOHN WESLEY POWELL

"The Ancient Province of Tusayan." *Scribner's* 11.2 (1875): 193–213.

The Exploration of the Colorado River and Its Canyons. Originally published as *Canyons of the Colorado*, 1895. New York: Dover, 1961.

Exploration of the Colorado River of the West and Its Tributaries Explored in 1869, 1870, 1871, and 1872, under the Direction of the Secretary of the Smithsonian Institution. Washington, DC: GPO, 1875.

"From Barbarism to Civilization." *American Anthropologist* 1 (1888): 97–123.

"From Savagery to Barbarism." *Anthropological Society of Washington—Transactions* 3 (1885): 173–96.

Geology of the Eastern Portion of the Uinta Mountains. Washington, DC: GPO, 1876.

"Institutions for the Arid Lands." *Century* 40 (1890): 111–16.

Introduction to the Study of Indian Languages. Washington, DC: GPO, 1877.

"The Irrigable Lands of the Arid Region." *Century* 39 (1890): 766–76.

"The Lesson of Conemaugh." *North American Review* 149 (1889): 150–56.

"The Non-Irrigable Lands of the Arid Region." *Century* 39 (1890): 915–22.

"An Overland Trip to the Grand Canyon." *Scribner's* 10 (1875): 659–78.

"Press Release." 1890 Water Resource Division of Records of Powell Survey Concerning Field Operations, 1889–1890. RG 57, Doc. #121. Washington, DC: National Archives.

Report on the Lands of the Arid Region of the United States with a More Detailed Account of the Lands of Utah. 1879. Facsimile edition with a new introduction by T. H. Watkins. Reprint, Harvard, MA: Harvard Common Press, 1983.

Report of Special Commissioners J. W. Powell and G. W. Ingalls on the Condition of the Ute Indians of Utah; The Paiutes of Utah… Washington, DC: GPO, 1874.

Report on the Geology of the Eastern Portion of the Uinta Mountains and a Region of Country Adjacent Thereto. Washington, DC: GPO, 1876.

Truth and Error or the Science of Intellection. Chicago: Open Court, 1898.

OTHER WORKS CITED

Abbey, Edward. *Desert Solitaire: A Season in the Wilderness.* 1968. Reprint, Layton, UT: Peregrine Smith Books, 1981.

———. *The Hidden Canyon: A River Journey.* New York: Viking, 1977.

———. *The Journey Home: Some Words in Defense of the American West.* New York: E. P. Dutton, 1977.

Adams, Eilean. *Hell or High Water: James White's Disputed Passage through the Grand Canyon, 1867.* Logan: Utah State University Press, 2001.

Alexander, Thomas G. *A Clash of Interests: Interior Department and Mountain West, 1863–96.* Provo: Brigham Young University Press, 1977.

Aton, James M. *Inventing John Wesley Powell: The Major, His Admirers and Cash-Register Dams in the Colorado River Basin.* Distinguished Faculty Lecture No. 9, Cedar City, UT: Southern Utah State College, 1988.

———. *John Wesley Powell.* Western Writers Series no. 114. Boise: Boise State University Press, 1994.

Baars, D. L. "Major John Wesley Powell, Colorado River Pioneer." *Geology and Natural History of the Fifth Field Conference, Powell Centennial River Expedition 1969.* Durango, CO: Four Corners Geological Society, 1969. 10–18.

Bartlett, Richard A. *The Great Surveys of the West.* Norman: University of Oklahoma Press, 1962.

———. "John Wesley Powell and the Great Surveys." *The American West: An Appraisal,* ed. Robert G. Ferris. Santa Fe: Museum of New Mexico Press, 1963. 48–67.

Berg, Peter, and Raymond Dasmann. "Reinhabiting California." In *Reinhabiting a Separate Country: A Bioregional Anthology of Northern California,* ed. Peter Berg. San Francisco: Planet Drum Books, 1978: 217–220.

Brewer, W. H. "John Wesley Powell." *American Journal of Science* 14 (1902): 377–82.

Bulger, Harold A. "First Man through the Grand Canyon." *Missouri Historical Society Bulletin* 17.4 (July 1961): 321–31.

Bureau of Reclamation. *Lake Powell: Jewel of the Colorado.* Washington DC:

GPO, 1965.

———. *Operation Glen Canyon: The Construction of Glen Canyon Dam*. Film. N.d.

Campbell, Joseph. *The Hero with a Thousand Faces*, 2nd ed. Princeton: Princeton University Press, 1968.

Cawelti, John G. *Adventure, Mystery and Romance: Formula Stories as Art and Popular Culture*. Chicago: University of Chicago Press, 1976.

Cline, Platt. Telephone interview by author. 20 January 1987.

Cohen, Michael P. *The Pathless Way: John Muir and American Wilderness*. Madison: University of Wisconsin Press, 1984.

Cooley, John, ed. *The Great Unknown: The Journals of the Historic First Expedition Down the Colorado River*. Flagstaff, AZ: Northland Publishing, 1988.

Darrah, William Culp. *Powell of the Colorado*. 1951. Reprint, Princeton: Princeton University Press, 1970.

———, ed. "The Exploration of the Colorado River in 1869" [includes journals of Powell, Bradley, Sumner]. *Utah Historical Quarterly* 15 (1947): 1–153.

Davis, William Morris. "Biographical Memoir of John Wesley Powell, 1834–1902." *National Academy of Sciences* 8 (February 1915): 11–83.

deBuys, William, ed. *Seeing Things Whole: The Essential John Wesley Powell*. Washington, DC: Island Press, 2004.

Dellenbaugh, Frederick. *A Canyon Voyage: The Narrative of the Second Powell Expedition Down the Green–Colorado River from Wyoming, and the Explorations on Land, in the Years 1871 and 1872*. 1908. Second edition. New Haven: Yale University Press, 1926.

———. *The Romance of the Colorado River: The Story of Its Discovery in 1540, With an Account of the Later Explorations, and with Special Reference to the Voyages of Powell Through the Line of Great Canyons*. New York and London: G.P. Putnam's Sons, 1902.

Department of the Interior. "1969 Centennial Will Honor Major John Wesley Powell." November 19, 1967. Page, Arizona. Glen Canyon National Recreation Area.

DeVoto, Bernard. *The Literary Fallacy*. 1944. Reprint, Port Washington, NY: Kennikat Press, 1969.

———. "Shall We Let Them Ruin Our National Parks?" *Saturday Evening Post* 223 (July 22, 1950): 17–19, 42–48.

Dutton, C. E. *Report on the Geology of the High Plateaus of Utah, with Atlas*. Washington, DC: GPO, 1880.

———. *Tertiary History of the Grand Cañon District, with Atlas*, Washington, DC: GPO, 1882.

Fernlund, Kevin J. *William Henry Holmes and the Rediscovery of the American West*. Albuquerque: University of New Mexico Press, 2000.

Foner, Philip S. ed. *Basic Writing of Thomas Jefferson*. New York: Willey Book Company, 1944.

Foster, Mike. *Strange Genius: The Life of Ferdinand Vandeveer Hayden*. Niwot, CO: Roberts Rinehart Publishers, 1994.

Fowler, Don D., ed. *"Photographed All the Best Scenery": Jack Hillers's Diary of the Powell Expeditions, 1871–1875*. Salt Lake City: University of Utah Press, 1972.

Fowler, Don D., and Catherine S. Fowler, eds. *Anthropology of the Numa: John Wesley Powell's Manuscripts on the Numic Peoples of Western North America, 1868–1880*. Washington, DC: Smithsonian Institution Press, 1971.

Ghiglieri, Michael P. *First through Grand Canyon: The Secret Journals and Letters of the 1869 Crew Who Explored the Green and Colorado Rivers*. Flagstaff, AZ: Puma Press, 2003.

Gilbert, Grove Karl. "John Wesley Powell." *Open Court* 17 (1903): 228–347.

_____. *Report on the Geology of the Henry Mountains*. Washington, DC: GPO, 1877.

———, et al. "John Wesley Powell." *Science* 16 (October 1902): 561–67, 781–90.

Goetzmann, William H., and William N. Goetzmann. *The West of the Imagination*. New York: W. W. Norton, 1986.

Harris, Marvin. *The Rise of Anthropological Theory: A History of Theories of Culture*. New York: Thomas Y. Crowell Co., 1968.

Harvey, Mark W. T. *A Symbol of Wilderness: Echo Park and the American Conservation Movement*. Albuquerque: University of New Mexico Press, 1994.

Haymond, Jay, and John F. Hoffman. "Interview with Otis R. 'Dock' Marston." May 1976. Utah State Historical Society, Salt Lake City.

Hays, Samuel. *Conservation and the Gospel of Efficiency: The Progressive Conservation Movement 1880–1920*. Cambridge: Harvard University Press, 1959.

Hundley, Norris. *Water and the West: The Colorado River Compact and the Politics of Water in the West*. Berkeley: University of California Press, 1975.

James, George Wharton. *Reclaiming the Arid West: The Story of the United States Reclamation Service*. New York: Dodd, Mead and Company, 1917.

Jones, Stan. *Glen Canyon Dam and Steel Arch Bridge*. Page, AZ: Sun Country Publications, 1984.

Judd, Neil M. *The Bureau of American Ethnology: A Partial History*. Norman: University of Oklahoma Press, 1967.

Larsen, Wesley P. "The Letter, or Were the Powell People Really Killed by Indians?" *Canyon Legacy* 17 (Spring 1993): 12–18.

LaRue, E. C. *The Colorado River and Its Utilization*. U.S. Geological Survey Water Supply Paper 395. Washington, DC: GPO, 1916.

———. *Water Power and Flood Control of Colorado River Below Green River, Utah*. U.S. Geological Survey Water Supply Paper 556. Washington, DC: GPO, 1925.

Lavender, David. *River Runners of the Grand Canyon*. Grand Canyon, AZ:

Grand Canyon Natural History Association, 1985.

Leydet, Francois. *Time and the River Flowing: Grand Canyon*. San Francisco: Sierra Club Books, 1964.

Limerick, Patricia Nelson. *Desert Passages: Encounters with the American Deserts*. Albuquerque: University of New Mexico Press, 1985.

Lincoln, Mrs. M. D. "John Wesley Powell." *Open Court* 16, 17 (Dec. 1902–Feb. 1903): 705–15, 14–25, 86–93.

Lowenthal, David. *The Past Is a Foreign Country*. Cambridge: Cambridge University Press, 1985.

Marston, Otis "Dock," ed. "The Lost Journal of John Colton Sumner." *Utah Historical Quarterly* 37 (Spring 1969): 173–89.

Meadows, Paul. *John Wesley Powell: Frontiersman of Science*. University of Nebraska Series 10. Lincoln: University of Nebraska, 1952.

Merrill, George P. "John Wesley Powell." *The American Geologist* 31 (June 1903): 327–33.

Miller, Peter, and Bruce Dale. "John Wesley Powell: Vision for the West." *National Geographic* 185 (April 1994): 89–115.

Morgan, Louis H. *Ancient Society: Or, Researches in the Lines of Human Progress from Savagery Through Barbarism to Civilization*. New York: H. Holt and Company, 1907.

Morris, Lindsey Gardner. "John Wesley Powell: Scientist and Educator." *Illinois State University Journal* 31.3 (Feb. 1969): 2–47.

Nash, Roderick. *Wilderness and the American Mind*, 3rd ed. New Haven: Yale University Press, 1982.

Newell, Frederick H. *Irrigation in the United States*, 3rd ed. New York: Thomas Y. Crowell Co., 1906.

Porter, Eliot. *The Place No One Knew: Glen Canyon on the Colorado*. San Francisco: Sierra Club Books, 1963.

Pyne, Stephen J. *Dutton's Point: An Intellectual History of the Grand Canyon*. Grand Canyon, AZ: Grand Canyon Natural History Association, 1982.

———. *Grove Karl Gilbert: A Great Engine of Research*. Austin: University of Texas Press, 1980.

———. *How the Canyon Became Grand: A Short History*. New York: Penguin Books, 1999.

Rabbitt, Mary C., et al. *The Colorado Region and John Wesley Powell*. U.S. Geological Survey Professional Paper 669. Washington, DC: GPO, 1969.

Reisner, Marc. *Cadillac Desert: The American West and Its Disappearing Water*. New York: Viking, 1986.

Robinson, Michael. *Water for the West: The Bureau of Reclamation 1902–1977*. Chicago: Public Works Historical Society, 1979.

Schmeckebier, Lawrence F. *Catalog and Index of the Hayden, King, Powell, and Wheeler Surveys*. U.S. Geological Survey Bulletin 222. Washington, DC: GPO, 1904.

Shabecoff, Philip. "U.S. Bureau for Water Projects Shifts Focus to Conservation." *New York Times*, 2 October 1987, p. 11.

Shepard, Paul. *Man in the Landscape: A Historic View of the Esthetics of Nature*. New York: Alfred A. Knopf, 1967.

Smith, Henry Nash. "Clarence King, John Wesley Powell, and the Establishment of the United States Geological Survey." *Mississippi Valley Historical Review* 34 (1947): 37–58.

———. *The Virgin Land: The American West as Symbol and Myth*. 1950. Reprint, Cambridge: Harvard University Press, 1978.

Smythe, William E. *The Conquest of Arid America*. 1899. Reprint, Seattle: University of Washington Press, 1969.

Spangler, Jerry D. "Paradigms and Perspectives Revisited: A Class I Overview of the Uinta Basin and Tavaputs Plateau." Report prepared for the Vernal office, Bureau of Land Management, 2002.

Stanton, Robert Brewster. *Colorado River Controversies*. 1932. Reprint, Boulder City, NV: Westwater Books, 1982.

Stegner, Wallace. *Beyond the Hundredth Meridian: John Wesley Powell and the Second Opening of the West*. 1954. Reprint, Lincoln: University of Nebraska Press, 1982.

———. *Clarence Edward Dutton: An Appraisal*. 1936. Reprint, Salt Lake City: University of Utah Press, 2005.

———. "Introduction." In *Report on the Lands of the Arid Region With a More Detailed Account of the Lands of Utah*, by John Wesley Powell. Cambridge: Belknap Press, 1962.

———. "Jack Sumner and John Wesley Powell." *Colorado Magazine* 26 (1949): 61–69.

Stephens, Hal G., and Eugene Shoemaker. *In the Footsteps of John Wesley Powell*. Boulder, CO: Johnson Books, 1987.

Sterling, Everett. "The Powell Irrigation Survey, 1888–1893." *Mississippi Valley Historical Review* 27 (1940): 421–34.

Stone, Julius F. *Canyon Country: The Romance of a Drop of Water and a Grain of Sand*. New York: G. P. Putnam's Sons, 1932.

Tatum, Stephen. *Inventing Billy the Kid: Visions of the Outlaw in America, 1881–1891*. Albuquerque: University of New Mexico Press, 1982.

Thomas, Marcia L. *John Wesley Powell: An Annotated Bibliography*. Westport, CT: Praeger, 2004.

Tobin, Gregory. *The Making of History: Walter Prescott Webb and "The Great Plains."* Austin: University of Texas Press, 1976.

Walcott, C. D. "John Wesley Powell." *24th Annual Report of the U.S.G.S. 1902–3*. Washington, DC: GPO, 1903, 271–87.

Warman, P. C. "Catalogue of the Published Writings of John Wesley Powell." *Proceedings of the Washington Academy of Sciences* 5 (18 July 1903): 131–87.

Warne, William E. *The Bureau of Reclamation*. New York: Praeger, 1973.

Webb, Walter Prescott. *The Great Plains*. 1931. Reprint, Lincoln: University of Nebraska Press, 1976.

White, Richard. "American Environmental History: The Development of a New Historical Field." *Pacific Historical Review* 54 (August 1985): 297–335.

Wibberley, Leonard. *Wes Powell: Conqueror of the Grand Canyon.* New York: Farrar, Straus, and Cudahy, 1958.

Worster, Donald. "History as Natural History: An Essay on Theory and Method." *Pacific Historical Review* 53 (February 1984): 1–19.

———. *Rivers of Empire: Water, Aridity and the Growth of the American West.* New York: Pantheon, 1985.

———. *A River Running West: The Life of John Wesley Powell.* New York: Oxford University Press, 2001.

———. *An Unsettled Country: Changing Landscapes of the American West.* Albuquerque: University of New Mexico Press, 1994.

Zernel, John J. "John Wesley Powell: Science and Reform in a Positive Context." PhD diss., Oregon State University, 1983.